No doubt about it—*Simplified G*  quickly become recommended re shine the light of Christ's Gospel clear, concise, and compelling language, author and lawyer David Hazelton opens up the letters of Paul and powerfully lets them speak not only into our individual Christian lives but into our corporate witness to a watching and ever-changing world. Simply outstanding!

HAROLD B. SMITH, PRESIDENT AND CEO, *CHRISTIANITY TODAY*

David Hazelton has a passion for God's Word and a gift for making it clear. Not only will his book help you understand Paul's letters to the churches, it will give you a firm grasp of the nature of the gospel and its implications for daily living. If you love God's Word, you will love this book.

JOHN KOESSLER, CHAIR AND PROFESSOR, DEPARTMENT OF PASTORAL STUDIES, MOODY BIBLE INSTITUTE; AUTHOR OF *TRUE DISCIPLESHIP: THE ART OF FOLLOWING JESUS* AND *THE SURPRISING GRACE OF DISAPPOINTMENT: FINDING HOPE WHEN GOD SEEMS TO FAIL US*

David fuses the incisive mind of a lawyer with the spiritual heart of a pastor-teacher to produce this highly readable and practical synthesis of Paul's instructions to the "ordinary Christians" of the first-century church. The Good News of the Gospel shines through every page and provides the touchstone of every facet of the Apostle's thought. Having seen David teach this material in our church over many years, I am delighted to see it now in print. May those who read it be as instructed and edified as those who have already heard it.

BILL KYNES, SENIOR PASTOR, CORNERSTONE EVANGELICAL FREE CHURCH

The Simplified Guide: Paul's Letters to the Churches is a clear, straightforward exploration of the Apostle's writings with direct, practical applications for daily living. Provoking the reader in every chapter to consider the life-changing nature of Paul's teaching, Hazelton's *Guide* can be profitably used for personal devotion or group study.

DR. DANIEL PAUL HORN, PROFESSOR, WHEATON COLLEGE

The Simplified Guide:
Paul's Letters to the Churches

The
Simplified Guide

Paul's Letters to the Churches

DAVID HAZELTON

Published by
Deep River Books
Sisters, Oregon
www.deepriverbooks.com

Published in association with literary agent David Jacobsen of D.C. Jacobson & Associates LLC, an author management company. www.dcjacobson.com.

ISBN-13: 9781937756840
ISBN-10: 193775684X

Library of Congress: 2013937429

Printed in the USA
Cover design by David Litwin, Purefusion Media
and Rhonda Funk

To my loving wife, Beky, and our three wonderful children,
Rex, Peter, and Katie.

To David, Mike, Lisa, Kit, Todd, Sue, Dan, Bill, Chrisi,
Sam, Will, Lowell, Bruce, Steve, and John, for your tremendous help
with drafts of this book.

And to the dozens of Bible study groups and Sunday School classes
that gave me the opportunity to teach on Paul's letters
over the past thirty-five years.

CONTENTS

CONCLUSION: YOUR OWN STUDY OF
PAUL'S LETTERS TO THE CHURCHES—211

INTRODUCTION

What does the word "gospel" bring to mind? Perhaps a music style, a preacher at a revival meeting, or some subculture within the broader Christian community. *Merriam Webster's Online Dictionary* offers several more substantive definitions including "the message concerning Christ, the kingdom of God and salvation," and more broadly "the message or teachings of a religious leader," or "something accepted as infallible truth or as a guiding principle of doctrine."

In the Bible, the Apostle Paul provides an even more specific and concrete description of the Christian gospel—one that centers on the person of Jesus Christ, his death on the cross, and his resurrection from the dead. Paul states plainly and forcefully:

> I want to remind you of the gospel I preached to you, which you received and on which you have taken your stand. By this gospel you are saved, if you hold firmly to the word I preached to you. Otherwise, you have believed in vain.

> For what I received I passed on to you as of first importance: that Christ died for our sins according to the Scriptures, that he was buried, that he was raised on the third day according to the Scriptures. (1 Cor. 15:1–4)

Paul further explains that "the gospel I preached is not of human origin. I did not receive it from any man, nor was I taught it; rather, I received it by revelation from Jesus Christ" (Gal. 1:11–12). He defined himself, his ministry and his message by the gospel that he received from Christ. He was "set apart for the gospel of God" and served "in my spirit in preaching the gospel of his Son" (Rom. 1:1, 9). He had "the priestly duty of proclaiming the gospel of God" (Rom. 15:16). He was sent by

Christ "to preach the gospel" (1 Cor. 1:17) and was "entrusted with the gospel" (1 Thess. 2:4). "I will fearlessly make known the mystery of the gospel, for which I am an ambassador in chains" (Eph. 6:19–20). "I am put here for the defense of the gospel" (Phil. 1:16).

The gospel was also central to Paul's instructions to the early Christians. Indeed, out of the ninety-four times that the word "gospel" appears in the Bible, seventy-seven come from the pen of Paul. The gospel is no less central for us today. In this book, we will be studying—and seeking to apply—Paul's instructions on gospel-centered living from his nine letters to the churches: Romans, 1 Corinthians, 2 Corinthians, Galatians, Ephesians, Philippians, Colossians, 1 Thessalonians, and 2 Thessalonians.

Paul's letters provide a remarkably consistent and coherent description of the gospel-centered life on matters of belief, behavior, and relationships. When discussing what we believe as Christians, Paul both begins with the gospel message and connects all of our core beliefs back to the gospel. And what we believe as followers of Christ provides the foundation for how we are to live. Without the power of the gospel, we cannot live the holy life to which we are called. And if we continue in our old, sinful patterns of conduct, we cannot develop the sorts of healthy relationships intended by God. A unified picture of the gospel-centered life emerges from Paul's practical instructions.

The Apostle Peter noted this consistency among Paul's letters, remarking that Paul "writes the same way in all his letters," using "the wisdom that God gave him" (2 Pet. 3:15–16). Significantly, even at the time of Peter's writing (around AD 65), he identified Paul's letters as part of the "Scriptures" (2 Pet. 3:16). While it is true that Paul wrote to believers in particular contexts, his instructions are based on God's eternal truths. Christians in every age struggle with the same basic challenges— issues of belief, behavior, and relationships. Paul addresses these thorny matters with practical and godly solutions based on hands-on wisdom.

Paul wrote to "all those everywhere who call on the name of our Lord Jesus Christ" (1 Cor. 1:2). His instructions were not directed primarily to theologians, pastors, or priests. He wrote to the whole church—

to regular Christians, like you and me—about the daily challenges that we confront in our walk with Christ. Far from dry works of abstract theology, Paul's letters provide practical instruction to people without any special theological training or educational credentials. Paul's passion is seeing every believer put the gospel into practice.

Rather than studying Paul's individual letters in isolation, we will be looking at all nine of his letters to the churches as a whole. There is a good reason for this approach.

Consider the difference between how you and a botanist might take a walk in the woods. The botanist might spend her time studying trees or flowers, perhaps examining an individual leaf or flower petal with a magnifying glass for hours on end. However, you would likely be more interested in enjoying your walk and hopefully gaining a better appreciation for the ecosystem as a whole. While the botanist is already an expert, an everyday hiker like you and me would benefit especially from a travel guide who identifies which trails to take, how to avoid danger, which plants are safe to eat, and so on. We need practical information to have a safe, positive, and productive hike!

We are going to walk through Paul's nine letters to the churches like we would take a walk through the woods. We could stop and examine the subtle nuances of each verse like a botanist might study an individual leaf. While there are great benefits to a chapter-by-chapter or verse-by-verse study of each of Paul's letters in isolation, we don't want to lose the forest for the trees. Therefore, on this particular walk, we will be trying to appreciate the overall beauty and logic in the spiritual ecosystem described by Paul. When we see the big picture, we can find our God-given place in it.

Our walk through Paul's letters will be guided by a few core principles. First and foremost, we will work hard to remain faithful to what Paul says. This travel guide reports Paul's words without extensive commentary. If you're an experienced traveler through Paul's letters, the terrain should look familiar. What may be new is how we collect what Paul says on a subject from each of his letters to give ourselves a better view of how his instructions fit together to form a living and practical whole.

Even a veteran hiker can benefit from this big picture approach to Paul's letters.

Second, this travel guide seeks to present everything that Paul says on each of our three subjects: Right Beliefs (chapters 1–5), Right Conduct (chapters 6–10), and Right Relationships (chapters 11–16). It collects Paul's practical instructions on specific issues as faithfully and completely as possible—rather than promoting a particular view or interpretation of his instructions. Readers therefore can make their own observations about applying Paul's instructions to their lives.

Third, it tries to be user friendly. The chapters are short and use a question-and-answer format so that we see clearly Paul's answers to specific questions. It is written to be a practical guide that can be read now and returned to later when a particular issue arises. At the end of each chapter, discussion questions will help us consider how to apply Paul's instructions to everyday life.

Let me offer another illustration. Imagine one of those 1,000-piece jigsaw puzzles. At first, the pieces seem like a hopeless mess, but as we study them we begin to sort them out based on subtle shadings of color or the shape of their edges. We gradually begin to see the big picture. There may be times when we can't seem to find the place for a particular piece, and while we might be tempted to toss out that piece, we know the picture won't be complete without it. We also shouldn't try to force a piece into a place it doesn't belong. And while we might be tempted to complete the picture with pieces from another puzzle box—or make up our own pieces—we know that the picture won't be right if we do.

Similarly, as we piece together Paul's instructions, we need to use all of the pieces that he provides. We need to fit them together patiently and look at the big picture. We need to resist the temptation to ignore or alter pieces provided by Paul. We also want to avoid adding pieces from outside the Scriptures—whether provided by others or by our own imagination. When we properly finish the puzzle and step back to look at it, we will see that Paul's letters provide a coherent picture of the gospel-centered life.

Before starting our walk—or beginning to work on our puzzle—

we'll pause briefly to consider Paul's call to proclaim Christ's gospel to the church, his personal ministry to local churches, and his letters to the churches as found in the Bible. Some hikers are so eager to get into the woods that they have little patience for the introductory comments, but we'll enjoy the journey more with a little background information.

Paul's Call to Proclaim the Gospel

Paul was a man of passion and action. Prior to his conversion, Paul's passion was directed against the church. He was dedicated to trying "to destroy the church. Going from house to house, he dragged off both men and women and put them in prison" (Acts 8:3). He was "breathing out murderous threats against the Lord's disciples" (Acts 9:1). There were "many reports about this man and all the harm he has done to your [Christ's] holy people in Jerusalem" (Acts 9:13). He sought "to do all that was possible to oppose the name of Jesus of Nazareth" (Acts 26:9). He "put many of the Lord's people in prison, and when they were put to death, I [Paul] cast my vote against them" (Acts 26:10). "I persecuted the followers of this Way to their death" (Acts 22:4). "I was so obsessed with persecuting them that I even hunted them down in foreign cities" (Acts 26:11). In short, Paul was waging all-out war on the church.

Paul viewed Christians as heretical blasphemers who proclaimed that Jesus was the Christ, the Savior of the world. Their beliefs seemed to conflict directly with what he had been taught as a faithful Jew. He was born into the tribe of Benjamin, circumcised on the eighth day, and trained as a Pharisee (Phil. 3:5). He received a strict religious education and studied under Gamaliel, a leading rabbi of that day (Acts 22:3). He "conformed to strictest sect of our [Jewish] religion" (Acts 26:5) and rigidly followed the Jewish law (Phil. 3:6). It took God's direct intervention for Paul to understand that Jesus Christ was, in fact, the fulfillment of everything he had been taught.

Jesus confronted Paul (also known as Saul) and turned his world upside down as he traveled to Damascus to continue his persecution of the church. Paul had gone "to the high priest and asked him for letters to the synagogues in Damascus, so that if he found any there who belonged to the Way, whether men or women, he might take them as prisoners to Jerusalem" (Acts 9:1–2). However:

> As he neared Damascus on his journey, suddenly a light from heaven flashed around him. He fell to the ground and heard a voice say to him, "Saul, Saul, why do you persecute me?"
>
> "Who are you, Lord?" Saul asked.
>
> "I am Jesus, whom you are persecuting," he replied. (Acts 9:3–5)

One of the most striking aspects of Jesus' words is that, rather than speaking of Paul's persecution of the *church*, Jesus asks, "Why do you persecute *me*" and identifies himself as "Jesus, whom you are persecuting." The identification of Jesus Christ with the church provides an important insight into Paul's ministry to the church for the rest of his life.

Paul always had been a man on a mission—but now his marching orders were coming from the very God whose followers he had been so keen to eradicate. At the time of Paul's conversion, Jesus declared: "This man is my chosen instrument to proclaim my name to the Gentiles and their kings and to the people of Israel" (Acts 9:15). This is a breathtaking statement: Jesus *chose* his worst enemy to represent him to the world.

Paul went away for three years following his conversion—first to Arabia and then Damascus—before going to Jerusalem to meet with the apostles Peter and James (Gal. 1:15–19). It appears that during this three-year period Paul received a direct revelation from Christ of the gospel message that he was to preach. In Galatians 1:11–12, he explains: "I want you to know, brothers and sisters, that the gospel I preached is not of human origin. I did not receive it from any man, nor was I taught it; rather, I received it by revelation from Jesus Christ." He refers to "the mystery made known to me by revelation" (Eph. 3:3). God's direct revelation to Paul is further suggested by 2 Corinthians 12:1–4 where Paul discusses his "visions and revelations from the Lord," including being "caught up to paradise" where he "heard inexpressible things." While Paul was a man of great learning and credentials, it was God's revelation to him—not Paul's own reasoning—that provides the foundation for his proclamation of the gospel.

While preaching the gospel to both Jew and non-Jew (or Gentile), Paul was called by God specifically to be "an apostle to the Gentiles" (Gal. 2:8). In Paul's words, "I had been entrusted with the task of preaching the gospel to the uncircumcised [Gentiles], just as Peter had been to the circumcised [Jews]" (Gal. 2:7). He was "a minister of Christ Jesus to the Gentiles" with "the priestly duty of proclaiming the gospel of God, so that the Gentiles might become an offering acceptable to God, sanctified by the Holy Spirit" (Rom. 15:16). He especially wanted to bring the gospel to people who had never heard of Jesus (2 Cor. 10:15–16). "It has always been my ambition to preach the gospel where Christ was not known" (Rom. 15:20). In his journeys, Paul travelled far and wide, proclaiming the gospel and establishing churches across the known world.

PAUL'S PERSONAL MINISTRY TO THE CHURCHES

Paul's home church—his point of departure for his three missionary journeys—was Antioch, the first city where a large number of Gentiles had put their faith in Christ (Acts 11:20–22). While Paul was not the first to bring the gospel to Antioch, he spent a year there during which he and Barnabas "met with the church and taught great numbers of people" (Acts 11:26). It was in Antioch where "the Holy Spirit said, 'Set apart for me Barnabas and Saul for the work to which I have called them.' So after they had fasted and prayed, they placed their hands on them and sent them off" (Acts 13:1–3).

The book of Acts reports Paul's missionary journeys in considerable detail. His first missionary journey is recorded in Acts 13:1 to 14:28, his second journey in Acts 15:36 to 18:22, and his third in Acts 18:23 to 21:17. The record of his fourth "missionary" journey, which was actually a trip to Rome as a prisoner following his arrest in Jerusalem, is found in Acts 21:18 to 28:31. Paul plays such a central role in Acts that he is identified by name well over 150 times—more than twice as often as any other apostle or member of the early church.

PAUL'S FIRST MISSIONARY JOURNEY

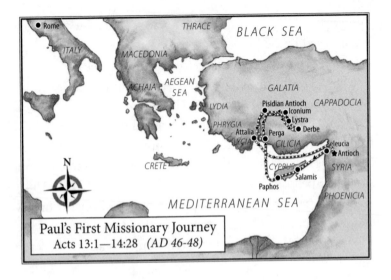

Paul's First Missionary Journey
Acts 13:1—14:28 *(AD 46-48)*

At the start of his first and shortest missionary journey, Paul travelled with Barnabas throughout the island of Cyprus proclaiming the gospel, before sailing to Perga (Acts 13:4–13). Then they took the gospel message to Pisidian Antioch, preaching first in the Jewish synagogue (Acts 13:14–43) as they had in Cyprus (Acts 13:4–5). Pisidian Antioch was located about 400 miles from the other Antioch, which served as Paul's home church. Both cities were named after the Syrian king Antiochus. When opposition arose in the synagogue in Pisidian Antioch (after initial enthusiasm and interest), they took the gospel to the Gentiles in that city (Acts 13:42–48). "The word of the Lord spread through the whole region" (Acts 13:49).

Paul and Barnabas next took the gospel message to Iconium (Acts 14:1–7), Lystra and Derbe (Acts 14:8–20). In Iconium, "they spoke so effectively that a great number of Jews and Greeks believed" (Acts 14:1). However, opposition also arose in Iconium (Acts 14:2, 5) and again in Lystra where "they stoned Paul and dragged him outside the city, thinking he was dead. But after the disciples had gathered around him, he got up and went back into the city" (Acts 14:19–20). He continued to preach the gospel and "returned to Lystra, Iconium and [Pisidian] Antioch, strengthening the disciples and encouraging them to remain true to the faith" (Acts 14:21–22). All of these cities—Pisidian Antioch, Iconium, Lystra, and Derbe—were located in what is believed to be the Roman province of Galatia, and they were likely among the churches to which Paul wrote his letter to the Galatians.

After passing through the regions of Pisidia and Pamphylia, as well as the cities of Perga and Attalia, Paul returned to his home church of Antioch (Acts 14:24–26). There he confronted false teachers who insisted: "Unless you are circumcised, according to the custom taught by Moses, you cannot be saved" (Acts 15:1). "So Paul and Barnabas were appointed, along with some other believers, to go up to Jerusalem to see the apostles and elders about this question" (Acts 15:2).

At the meeting of the apostles and elders in Jerusalem, Peter spoke forcefully against this false teaching and concluded:

Now then, why do you try to test God by putting on the necks of the Gentiles a yoke that neither we nor our ancestors have been able to bear? No! We believe it is through the grace of our Lord Jesus that we are saved, just as they are. (Acts 15:10–11)

Paul, Barnabas and James also spoke against any requirement for circumcision, citing both the authority of Scripture and their witness of God's work among the Gentiles (Acts 15:12–18). As a result, "the apostles and elders, with the whole church, decided to choose some of their own men and send them to Antioch with Paul and Barnabas" (Acts 15:22) to convey the decision rejecting the false teaching that circumcision was necessary for salvation (Acts 15:23–29).

Paul's letter to the Galatians was likely written about this time. It confronts many of the same issues addressed at the council in Jerusalem. Like the Jerusalem council, Paul's letter to the Galatians rejects emphatically the false teaching that Christians had to be circumcised and follow the Old Testament law. This letter is probably the first of Paul's epistles.

PAUL'S SECOND MISSIONARY JOURNEY

During his second missionary journey, Paul—accompanied this time by Silas rather than Barnabas—set out from Antioch and traveled "through Syria and Cilicia, strengthening the churches" (Acts 15:35–41). They "traveled from town to town," returning to Derbe, Lystra and apparently Iconium in the province of Galatia, and "delivered the decisions reached by the apostles and elders in Jerusalem" (Acts 16:1-4). "So the churches were strengthened in the faith and grew daily in numbers" (Acts 16:5).

After Paul travelled "throughout the region of Phrygia and Galatia," God revealed in a vision that he should go to the region of Macedonia to preach the gospel (Acts 16:6–10). He obediently preached the gospel in the Macedonian cities of Philippi (Acts 16:11–40), Thessalonica (Acts 17:1–9) and Berea (Acts 17:10–14). Paul met extreme opposition in Philippi. He and Silas were seized, stripped, beaten and imprisoned (Acts 16:16–24). Through God's miraculous intervention, they were released from prison and allowed to continue on their way (Acts 16:25–40).

In Thessalonica, some believed the gospel, but the opposition of others resulted in Paul leaving that city (Acts 17:5). While Paul clearly wanted to return, it does not appear that he was able. He explained in 1 Thessalonians 2:17–18 that: "But, brothers and sisters, when we were orphaned by being separated from you for a short time (in person, not in thought), out of our intense longing we made every effort to see you. For we wanted to come to you—certainly I, Paul, did, again and again—but Satan blocked our way."

Paul next sailed to Greece where his first stop was Athens (Acts 17:15–34). While "some of the people became followers" (Acts 17:34), it does not appear that Paul's visit to Athens had much of an immediate effect. After leaving Athens, he spent some time in Corinth where he preached to the Jews and then the Gentiles (Acts 18:1–18). There, "many of the Corinthians who heard Paul believed and were baptized" (Acts 18:8).

During this period, Paul probably wrote both 1 Thessalonians and 2 Thessalonians. In 1 Thessalonians 3:1–2, Paul refers to his stay in Athens and to sending Timothy back to care for the Thessalonians. Since Timothy was with Paul when he wrote both letters to the Thessalonians (1 Thess. 1:1; 2 Thess. 1:1), and since Timothy rejoined Paul while in Corinth (Acts 18:5), he likely wrote both letters from Corinth in response to news reported by Timothy.

Paul next stopped briefly in Ephesus and left there two coworkers, Priscilla and Aquila, who had accompanied him from Corinth. They continued the work in Ephesus while Paul returned to Antioch, thus ending his second missionary journey (Acts 18:19–22).

Paul's Third Missionary Journey

Paul's Third Missionary Journey
Acts 18:23—21:17 (AD 53-57)

During his third missionary journey, Paul returned to many of the places where he previously preached the gospel. "After spending some time in Antioch, Paul set out from there and traveled from place to place throughout the region of Galatia and Phrygia, strengthening all the disciples" (Acts 18:23). He then returned to Ephesus—this time spending more than two years (Acts 19:8–10)—where "God did extraordinary miracles through Paul, so that even handkerchiefs and aprons that had touched him were taken to the sick, and their illnesses were cured and the evil spirits left them" (Acts 19:11–12).

As a result of his preaching in Ephesus, "all the Jews and Greeks who lived in the province of Asia heard the word of the Lord" (Acts 19:10). With this great success came extreme opposition, including a riot directed against the Ephesian Christians (Acts 19:23–41). Paul probably wrote 1 Corinthians while in Ephesus before leaving for Macedonia after the riot ended (Acts 20:1; 1 Cor. 16:5–9).

Upon arriving in Macedonia, Paul "traveled through that area, speaking many words of encouragement to the people, and finally arrived in Greece, where he stayed three months" (Acts 20:2–3). Paul indicates that he wrote 2 Corinthians while in Macedonia (2 Cor. 2:13; 7:5). One of the Macedonian cities to which Paul returned was Philippi (Acts 20:6). While Acts contains no record that he ever returned again to Ephesus, Paul did send for the elders of that church to meet him in Miletus where he provided personal and passionate instruction on caring for the church (Acts 20:17–38).

At that time, Paul was in a hurry to return to Jerusalem (Acts 20:16) explaining: "And now, compelled by the Spirit, I am going to Jerusalem, not knowing what will happen to me there. I only know that in every city the Holy Spirit warns me that prison and hardships are facing me" (Acts 20:22–23). Paul headed to Jerusalem despite prophetic warnings during his stops in Tyre and Caesarea about the trouble he would meet (Acts 21:1–16). Suggesting that he wrote Romans at about this time, Paul explains in Romans 15:25–26: "I am on my way to Jerusalem in the service of the Lord's people there. For Macedonia and Achaia were pleased to make a contribution for the poor among the Lord's people in

Jerusalem." After delivering this contribution to the needy in Jerusalem, Paul's plan was to take the gospel to Spain and, on his way there, to stop by Rome (Rom. 15:23–24, 28–29). Paul did go to Rome later, but as a prisoner.

PAUL'S JOURNEY TO ROME

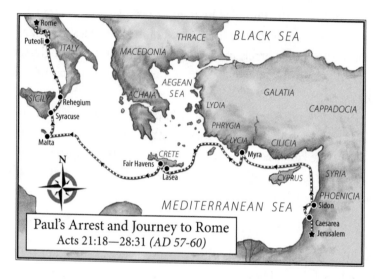

Paul's final journey recorded in Acts began with his arrest in Jerusalem (Acts 21:27–36), then a show-trial before the Sanhedrin (Acts 22:30–23:11), a plot to kill him in Jerusalem (Acts 23:12–22), his transfer to the city of Caesarea to appear before Governor Felix who left Paul in prison for more than two years (Acts 23:23–24:27), another show-trial in Caesarea before Felix's successor Festus (Acts 25:1–12), yet another show-trial in Caesarea before King Agrippa (Acts 25:13–26:32), a trip to Rome as a prisoner on a ship that was wrecked during a violent storm (Acts 27:1–44), being washed ashore on the island of Malta where they stayed for three months (Acts 28:1–11), and finally catching another ship to Rome where Paul was kept under house arrest for two years (Acts 28:11–31).

Despite the dire circumstances of this journey, Paul continued to faithfully preach the gospel. He shared it with the crowd in Jerusalem following his arrest (Acts 21:37–22:21). His testimony before Governor Felix (Acts 24:10–21) and King Agrippa (Acts 26:1–29) are two of Paul's lengthiest sermons recorded in the book of Acts. Shortly after his arrival in Rome, he also called together the Jewish leaders to share the gospel with them (Acts 28:17–28). "He witnessed to them from morning till evening, explaining about the kingdom of God, and from the Law of Moses and from the Prophets he tried to persuade them about Jesus" (Acts 28:23). The final verse in the book of Acts provides the following report on Paul: "He proclaimed the kingdom of God and taught about the Lord Jesus Christ—with all boldness and without hindrance!" (Acts 28:31).

Paul's letters to the Ephesians, Philippians and Colossians are often called "prison epistles" because they are generally believed to have been written while Paul was a prisoner in Rome. In those letters, he expressly identifies himself as a "prisoner" or "in chains" (Eph. 3:1; 4:1; 6:20; Phil. 1:13–14; Col. 4:3, 18).

POSSIBILITY OF OTHER MISSIONARY JOURNEYS

The book of Acts does not record every moment of Paul's ministry. For example, while we know from Paul's letters that he visited Corinth at least twice and planned a third visit (2 Cor. 12:14; 13:1), Acts refers to only one visit by Paul to Corinth (Acts 18:1–18). These additional visits to Corinth apparently occurred during the period covered by Acts, but, for one reason or another, they are not mentioned in that account.

Paul may also have gone on missionary journeys after the events recorded in Acts. This possibility is suggested in Titus 1:5, where Paul states to his coworker Titus that "The reason I left you in Crete was that you might put in order what was left unfinished and appoint elders in every town, as I directed you." While the ship transporting Paul as a prisoner to Rome apparently stopped in Crete (Acts 27:7–8), Acts contains no mention of his preaching the gospel in Crete or working there with Titus. Perhaps he helped to establish a church in Crete after his release from house arrest in Rome.

Further suggesting the possibility of other journeys after the events recorded in Acts, Paul expressed confidence that he would one day take the gospel to Spain (Rom. 15:28–29), that he would visit Colosse (Philemon 22), and that he would spend the winter in Nicopolos (Titus 3:12). None of these events are recorded in Acts.

One possibility is that Paul was released from house arrest in Rome, resumed his travels spreading the gospel, and was later imprisoned again in Rome where he was martyred. Paul may have written Titus and 1 Timothy after his release from house arrest in Rome. Second Timothy may well have been his final letter, written while he was awaiting execution. In that letter, Paul identifies himself as a prisoner in chains (2 Tim. 1:8, 16) who was largely abandoned (2 Tim. 1:15; 4:9–11, 16). Reflecting that his life on earth was coming to an end, Paul explains:

> For I am already being poured out like a drink offering, and the time for my departure is near. I have fought the good fight, I have finished the race, I have kept the faith. Now there is in store for me the crown of righteousness, which the Lord, the righteous Judge, will award to me on that day—and not only to me, but also to all who have longed for his appearing. (2 Tim. 4:6–8)

The bottom line is that, while we do not know all the details of Paul's life and ministry, we do know that he remained faithful to the end to the person and gospel of Jesus Christ.

PAUL'S LETTERS IN THE NEW TESTAMENT

Although Paul is specifically named as the author in thirteen of the New Testament's twenty-seven books, it is easy to miss this fact because none of them are named after him. While many New Testament books are named after their authors, Paul's letters are named after the people to whom he wrote. The table of contents of the New Testament would look very different—and a little monotonous—if all of Paul's letters had been named after him. The following "table of contents" reflects such an approach (with the actual names of Paul's letters identified in parentheses):

Matthew	10 Paul (1 Timothy)
Mark	11 Paul (2 Timothy)
Luke	12 Paul (Titus)
John	13 Paul (Philemon)
Acts	Hebrews
1 Paul (Romans)	James
2 Paul (I Corinthians)	1 Peter
3 Paul (2 Corinthians)	2 Peter
4 Paul (Galatians)	1 John
5 Paul (Ephesians)	2 John
6 Paul (Philippians)	3 John
7 Paul (Colossians)	Jude
8 Paul (1 Thessalonians)	Revelation
9 Paul (2 Thessalonians)	

No other New Testament author wrote close to as many as Paul's thirteen books. By way of comparison, John wrote five books: the Gospel according to John, three epistles (1, 2 and 3 John), and the book of Revelation. Peter wrote two books: 1 and 2 Peter. Luke also wrote two books: the Gospel according to Luke and the book of Acts. Four other New Testament authors (Matthew, Mark, James and Jude) wrote a single book, each of which bears the author's name. The book of Hebrews does not identify the author and, through the centuries, several names have been suggested including Paul. Ironically, although Paul wrote nearly as many as of the New Testament's books as all others combined, not a single one is named after him.

Paul's letters are divided into the two groups based on whether he was writing to a church or an individual:

PAUL'S NINE LETTERS TO CHURCHES	PAUL'S FOUR LETTERS TO INDIVIDUALS
Romans	1 Timothy
1 Corinthians	2 Timothy
2 Corinthians	Titus
Galatians	Philemon
Ephesians	
Philippians	
Colossians	
1 Thessalonians	
2 Thessalonians	

His letters to the churches appear first and are followed immediately by his letters to individuals. Within Paul's letters to the churches, the order does not appear to be based on their dates or thematic principles. Instead, Paul's letters to the churches are generally organized from longest (Romans) to shortest (2 Thessalonians), with letters written to the same church grouped together (1 and 2 Corinthians, and 1 and 2 Thessalonians).

While our study focuses on Paul's instructions in his nine letters to the churches, it does refer occasionally to Paul's other letters (as well as other portions of the Bible) that seem particularly relevant to issues addressed in his letters to the churches. Paul's "pastoral epistles"—1 Timothy, 2 Timothy and Titus—were written to Paul's coworkers who helped plant churches. While these epistles are addressed to church planters rather than the "regular" Christians in the churches, they discuss some of the same issues as Paul's general epistles. Paul's letters to his fellow church planters thus provide a helpful perspective on several of the issues that he addresses in his letters to the general church membership.

With this background, we're now ready for our walk through Paul's nine letters to the churches. Our journey begins with Paul's instructions on the fundamental truths underlying our Christian faith. Part I is thus entitled "Right Beliefs." Building on a proper understanding of the gospel message, Part II (entitled "Right Conduct") discusses Paul's instructions on how we are to live as Christians. His instructions on Right Conduct have practical meaning only in light of his instructions on Right Beliefs. Part III (entitled "Right Relationships") explores Paul's instructions on how to build healthy relationships as intended by God. These relationships are possible only if our lives are being transformed by the gospel message of salvation (as discussed in Parts I and II). As we will see, Paul's instructions fit together to form a coherent and practical picture of how, as followers of Christ, we are to live gospel-centered lives.

Part I: Right Beliefs

Paul explains the essentials of the gospel message of salvation in simple and straightforward terms. Rather than focusing on a rigid set of rules, or a detailed set of rituals, or a complex system of theology, Paul focuses on the person of Jesus Christ, his death on the cross, and his resurrection from the dead. If we understand the gospel correctly, everything else will follow. Before we worry about any other issue, Paul wants us to understand the gospel in all of its clarity, beauty and majesty.

We therefore begin in chapter 1 with Paul's explanation of this pure and simple gospel. Due to its central importance, Paul issues strong warnings against any additions to or subtractions from this gospel as discussed chapter 2. While insisting on strict faithfulness to the essentials of the gospel, chapter 3 discusses Paul's declaration of our freedom in practices and personal convictions on secondary matters. Chapter 4 next explains that Paul relies on Scripture as the foundation for understanding the gospel and, more generally, what we believe as Christians. In chapter 5, we conclude Part I of our study by discussing how Paul takes a practical approach to "theological" issues, which brings us back, again and again, to the gospel.

CHAPTER 1

The Pure and Simple Gospel

This is the most important chapter in this book. As Paul makes clear, the gospel is the basis for our salvation. It is the foundation on which all of his other instructions are built. If we build on any other foundation, everything else that we believe or do will crumble in the end.

The gospel message as declared by Paul is easy to understand but often hard to accept. Almost everyone can readily grasp the essential elements of the gospel at a basic level. But many want to make it more complex than it is, perhaps because it is difficult to accept that something so important can be so simple. Paul is very clear, however, that the gospel message of salvation is simple, straightforward, and available to all who come in faith. Let's examine the foundation for Paul's teaching—and our faith—and what it means for us today.

WHAT ARE THE ESSENTIALS OF THE GOSPEL MESSAGE OF SALVATION?

In 1 Corinthians 15:1–4, Paul states plainly the gospel by which we are saved:

> I want to remind you of the gospel I preached to you, which you received and on which you have taken your stand. By this gospel you are saved, if you hold firmly to the word I preached to you. Otherwise, you have believed in vain.

> For what I received I passed on to you as of first importance: that Christ died for our sins according to the Scriptures, that he was buried, that he was raised on the third day according to the Scriptures.

Paul provides quite a buildup before identifying the essentials of the gospel message. "By this gospel you are saved" (1 Cor. 15:2). It is the "gospel I preached to you," the gospel "you received and on which you have taken your stand," the gospel to which you must "hold firmly," and it is a matter of "first importance" (1 Cor. 15:3). Having emphasized its importance, Paul states the essential elements of the gospel in a few simple words: "Christ died for our sins according to the Scriptures, that he was buried, that he was raised on the third day according to the Scriptures" (2 Cor. 15:3–4). Clearly, nothing is more important to Paul than the person of Jesus Christ, his death, and his resurrection.

The book of Acts documents that Paul preached this very gospel message to the churches when he was with them in person. When arriving in a city, it was the "custom" of Paul to go to the synagogue where "he reasoned with them from the Scriptures, explaining and proving that the Messiah had to suffer and rise from the dead. 'This Jesus I am proclaiming to you is the Messiah,' he said" (Acts 17:2–3). Thus, in his sermon recorded in Acts 13:13–41, Paul presented the "message of salvation" (v. 26) and "the good news" (v. 32) by focusing on the historic events of Jesus Christ's death and resurrection. Specifically, he proclaimed:

> The people of Jerusalem and their rulers did not recognize Jesus, yet in condemning him they fulfilled the words of the prophets that are read every Sabbath. Though they found no proper ground for a death sentence, they asked Pilate to have him executed. When they had carried out all that was written about him, they took him down from the cross and laid him in a tomb. But God raised him from the dead, and for many days he was seen by those who had traveled with him from Galilee to Jerusalem. (Acts 13:27–31)

Similarly, when put on trial for preaching the gospel, Paul explained: "I am saying nothing beyond what the prophets and Moses said would happen—that the Messiah would suffer and, as the first to rise from the dead, would bring the message of light to his own people and to the Gentiles" (Acts 26:22–23). We are often tempted to complicate the gospel, but when his back was to the wall, Paul stood firm on a simple statement about Jesus Christ, his death, and his resurrection.

Paul's insistence on this pure and simple gospel wasn't limited to his preaching. In his letters to the churches, Paul repeats again and again the simple gospel that he had preached. In 1 Corinthians 2:1–2, he explains: "When I came to you, I did not come with eloquence or human wisdom as I proclaimed to you the testimony about God. For I resolved to know nothing while I was with you except Jesus Christ and him crucified." Similarly, Paul declares in 1 Corinthians 1:23 that "we preach Christ crucified." He identifies "the message concerning faith that we proclaim: If you declare with your mouth, 'Jesus is Lord,' and believe in your heart that God raised him from the dead, you will be saved" (Rom. 10:8–9).

When describing the message that he preached to the Galatians, Paul declared: "Before your very eyes, Jesus Christ was clearly portrayed as crucified" (Gal. 3:1). Again, in 2 Timothy 2:8, Paul instructs: "Remember Jesus Christ, raised from the dead, descended from David. This is my gospel."

WHAT IS THE SIGNIFICANCE OF THE CRUCIFIXION OF JESUS CHRIST?

Jesus was crucified by the Romans, a regional empire that occupied and controlled Palestine at the time. It seemed like a matter of local politics in a back-water province, where the local Roman governor—a man named Pilate—sought to placate Jewish religious leaders who had a vendetta against Jesus. Yet there was a much deeper meaning to the crucifixion of Jesus—a God-ordained plan to restore the relationship between humans and their Creator, a relationship that was fractured when sin entered the world. It was this deeper, divine plan that compelled Paul.

In his death on the cross, Jesus Christ—who lived a life without sin—took our sin upon himself and accepted the punishment that we deserved. As Paul explains in Romans 5:6–11:

> You see, at just the right time, when we were still powerless, Christ died for the ungodly. Very rarely will anyone die for a righteous person, though for a good person someone might possibly dare to die. But God demonstrates his own love for us in this: While we were still sinners, Christ died for us.

> Since we have now been justified by his blood, how much more shall we be saved from God's wrath through him! For if, while we were God's enemies, we were reconciled to him through the death of his Son, how much more, having been reconciled, shall we be saved through his life! Not only is this so, but we also boast in God through our Lord Jesus Christ, through whom we have now received reconciliation.

Paul addresses this spiritual reality again and again in Romans, which contains his most in-depth discussion of the gospel and its implications for our lives. After explaining in Romans 1:18 to 3:20 that every person is a sinner who is without excuse before God and under God's wrath, Paul declares that we have access to forgiveness through Christ's death on the cross:

> For all have sinned and fall short of the glory of God, and all are justified freely by his grace through the redemption that came by Christ Jesus. God presented Christ as a sacrifice of atonement, through the shedding of his blood—to be received by faith. (Rom. 3:23–25)

To ensure that his readers understood the eternal significance of the crucifixion, Paul returns to it again and again. Romans 4:25 states: "He was delivered over to death for our sins and was raised to life for our justification." In Romans 6:6–7, we read: "For we know that our old self was crucified with him so that the body ruled by sin might be done away with, that we should no longer be slaves to sin—because anyone who has died has been set free from sin."

The life-changing power of Christ's atoning death is emphasized in Paul's other letters as well. Ephesians 1:7 explains: "In him we have redemption through his blood, the forgiveness of sins, in accordance with the riches of God's grace." In Colossians 2:13–14, Paul declares again that "you were dead in your sins" but:

> God made you alive with Christ. He forgave us all our sins, having canceled the charge of our legal indebtedness, which stood against us and condemned us; he has taken it away, nailing it to the cross.

Thus, as Paul states emphatically, the fact that "Christ died for our sins according to the Scriptures" is a matter of "first importance" (1 Cor. 15:3) because his death provides the basis for God's forgiveness of our sins.

WHAT IS THE SIGNIFICANCE OF JESUS CHRIST'S RESURRECTION FROM THE DEAD?

We humans are afraid of countless things. We fear spiders, clowns, heights, public spaces, public speaking, and a thousand other terrors. From the silly to the serious, fear is an unavoidable part of what it means to be human.

Yet there is one fear that rises like a specter above all others, that sounds a sinister echo in the background of our daily lives: the fear of death. Nothing is so terrifying as the realization that we will, sooner or later, die and confront the uncertainty about what will happen to us on the other side of this life. The inevitability of death makes it no easier to accept; its permanence forces us to come to grips with fundamental issues.

It is in this profoundly human context that Christ died as a man, just as every man, woman and child will eventually die. Yet Christ conquered death through his resurrection. As sons and daughters of God, we share in Christ's victory over death and his promise of eternal life.

Paul's most extensive discussion of the significance of Christ's resurrection is in 1 Corinthians 15:12–57. In that passage, he begins by correcting those who deny the resurrection, explaining that "if Christ has not been raised, our preaching is useless and so is your faith" (v. 14) and "if Christ has not been raised, your faith is futile; you are still in your sins" (v. 17). He then declares in verses 20–22:

> But Christ has indeed been raised from the dead, the firstfruits of those who have fallen asleep. For since death came through a man, the resurrection of the dead comes also through a man. For as in Adam all die, so in Christ all will be made alive.

On the day of our resurrection to eternal life, our decaying material bodies will be exchanged for glorified and imperishable bodies. Christ "will transform our lowly bodies so that they will be like his glorious body" (Phil. 3:21). Much as a seed is planted or sown in one form but then emerges from the earth as something new and better, Paul explains:

> So will it be with the resurrection of the dead. The body that is sown is perishable, it is raised imperishable; it is sown in dishonor, it is raised in glory; it is sown in weakness, it is raised in power; it is sown a natural body, it is raised a spiritual body. If there is a natural body, there is also a spiritual body. (1 Cor. 15:42–44)

He compares our current mortal bodies to "jars of clay" (2 Cor. 4:7) and an "earthly tent" which we will exchange for "an eternal house in heaven" (2 Cor. 5:1). The glory of what God has in store for us is beyond our comprehension. "'What no eye has seen, what no ear has heard, and what no human mind has conceived'—the things God has prepared for those who love him" (1 Cor. 2:9).

This resurrection power not only has eternal significance, it also has the power to transform our lives today. Emphasizing the connection between the resurrection and the power to live a holy life today, Paul explains in Romans 6:4–10 that:

> We were therefore buried with him through baptism into death in order that, just as Christ was raised from the dead through the glory of the Father, we too may live a new life. For if we have been united with him in a death like his, we will certainly also be united with him in a resurrection like his. For we know that our old self was crucified with him so that the body ruled by sin might be done away with, that we should no longer be slaves to sin—because anyone who has died has been set free from sin. Now if we died with Christ, we believe that we will also live with him. For we know that since Christ was raised from the dead, he cannot die again; death no longer has mastery over him. The death he died, he died to sin once for all; but the life he lives, he lives to God.

Again, Paul explains in Romans 8:11 that: "If the Spirit of him who raised Jesus from the dead is living in you, he who raised Christ from the dead will also give life to your mortal bodies because of his Spirit who lives in you."

Jesus Christ took our sins upon himself when he was crucified on the cross, but it was his glorious resurrection that conquered death and prepared the way for our resurrection and eternal life. The great human fear of death is conquered in the triumphant resurrection of Christ. His victory over death changed everything.

WHO IS JESUS CHRIST THAT HIS DEATH AND RESURRECTION COULD HAVE THIS SIGNIFICANCE?

Paul emphasizes the primary importance of the death and resurrection of Jesus Christ in all his teaching. Yet crucifixions were all too common during that period of human history. And while resurrections were exceedingly rare, the Bible records others such as Lazarus who were raised from the dead. What was it about Jesus Christ that, above anyone else who ever lived, his crucifixion and resurrection could have such eternal and earthshaking significance?

Paul states the answer plainly in Colossians 2:9: "For in Christ all the fullness of the Deity lives in bodily form." While Jesus "as to his earthly life was a descendant of David" (Rom. 1:3), he is also "in very nature God" (Phil. 2:6). He "is the image of the invisible God" (Col. 1:15). Detailing several of the fundamental characteristics that distinguish Jesus Christ from the rest of humanity, Paul continues in Colossians 1:15–20:

> The Son is the image of the invisible God, the firstborn over all creation. For in him all things were created: things in heaven and on earth, visible and invisible, whether thrones or powers or rulers or authorities; all things have been created through him and for him. He is before all things, and in him all things hold together. And he is the head of the body, the church; he is the beginning and the firstborn from among the dead, so that in everything he might have the supremacy. For God was pleased to have all his fullness dwell in him, and through him to reconcile to himself all things, whether things on earth or things in heaven, by making peace through his blood, shed on the cross.

In Ephesians 1:19–21, Paul explains how God's "incomparably great power" was demonstrated when God raised Christ from the dead and "seated him at his right hand in the heavenly realms, far above all rule and authority, power and dominion, and every name that is invoked, not only in the present age but also in the one to come." Paul continues in verses 22 and 23: "And God placed all things under his feet and appointed him to be head over everything for the church, which is his body, the fullness of him who fills everything in every way."

As declared by Paul, Jesus Christ's unique nature as sinless God who became man is the reason why his death could pay the price for our sins and thus provide the basis for our salvation. Outside of Jesus, there has never been a death that could provide forgiveness for our sins, and there has never been a resurrection that could conquer death and pave the way for our resurrection.

HOW DO WE RECEIVE THE GIFTS OF FORGIVENESS AND ETERNAL LIFE AVAILABLE THROUGH THE GOSPEL?

Christ paid the price for our forgiveness and conquered death so we could have eternal life. We are helpless without him. Salvation is therefore a gift received freely in faith, not something we earn through good works. Paul's letter to the Romans again contains his most systematic discussion of the role of faith in receiving salvation through the gospel. Emphasizing this important distinction between faith and works, he declares in Romans 4:4–5 that:

> Now to the one who works, wages are not credited as a gift but as an obligation. However, to the one who does not work but trusts God who justifies the ungodly, their *faith* is credited as righteousness.

Paul emphasizes the important role of faith for salvation again and again in Romans. "For in the gospel the righteousness of God is revealed—a righteousness that is by *faith* from first to last, just as it is written: 'The righteous will live by *faith*'" (Rom. 1:17). "This righteousness is given through *faith* in Jesus Christ to all who believe" (Rom. 3:22). Explaining that we "are justified freely by his [God's] grace through the redemption that came by Christ Jesus," Paul declares that "God presented Christ as a sacrifice of atonement, through the shedding of his blood—

to be received by *faith*" (Rom. 3:24–25). "For we maintain that a person is justified by *faith* apart from the works of the law" (Rom. 3:28). "Therefore, since we have been justified through *faith*, we have peace with God through our Lord Jesus Christ, through whom we have gained access by *faith* into this grace in which we now stand" (Rom. 5:1–2).

Driving the point home that faith has always been the basis by which people are justified before God, Paul points in Romans 4 to Abraham, the forefather of the Jews who lived more than 2,000 years before Christ's crucifixion, as a model of someone justified by faith. "'Abraham believed God, and it was credited to him as righteousness'" (Rom. 4:3). "Against all hope, Abraham in hope believed" in God's promise that he would be the father of many nations (Rom. 4:18). "Without weakening in his faith, he faced the fact that his body was as good as dead—since he was about a hundred years old" (Rom. 4:19). "Yet he did not waver through unbelief regarding the promise of God, but was strengthened in his faith and gave glory to God, being fully persuaded that God had power to do what he had promised. This is why 'it was credited to him as righteousness'" (Rom. 4:20–22).

Paul is emphatic that salvation in Christ must be received in faith. Indeed, in Romans and his other letters to the churches, he refers to "faith" more than 100 times. For example: "We live by *faith*, not by sight" (2 Cor. 5:7). "The life I now live in the body, I live by *faith* in the Son of God, who loved me and gave himself for me" (Gal. 2:20). "Clearly no one who relies on the law is justified before God, because 'the righteous will live by *faith*'" (Gal. 3:11). "He redeemed us in order that the blessing given to Abraham might come to the Gentiles through Christ Jesus, so that by *faith* we might receive the promise of the Spirit" (Gal. 3:14). "In him [Jesus] and through *faith* in him we may approach God with freedom and confidence" (Eph. 3:12).

In his personal testimony, Paul declares that he is found "not having a righteousness of my own that comes from the law, but that which is through *faith* in Christ—the righteousness that comes from God on the basis of *faith*" (Phil. 3:9). This small sampling of Paul's references to "faith" reflects his conviction that Christ has done it all, that we cannot save ourselves, and that we only can accept salvation in Christ through faith.

Perhaps the best definition of "faith" is found in the New Testament book of Hebrews. "Now faith is confidence in what we hope for and assurance about what we do not see" (Heb. 11:1). "And without faith it is impossible to please God, because anyone who comes to him must believe that he exists and that he rewards those who earnestly seek him" (Heb. 11:6). Unless received in faith, the gospel message has little meaning for the one who hears it. "For we also have had the good news proclaimed to us, just as they did; but the message they heard was of no value to them, because they did not share the faith of those who obeyed" (Heb. 4:2).

Faith does not require that we understand the mystery of the gospel in its fullness to accept it. When explaining "the message concerning faith that we proclaim," Paul states the simplicity of the expression of faith required for salvation:

> If you declare with your mouth, "Jesus is Lord," and believe in your heart that God raised him from the dead, you will be saved. For it is with your heart that you believe and are justified, and it is with your mouth that you profess your faith and are saved. (Rom. 10:8–10)

When we genuinely believe in our hearts and confess with our mouths, it is the Spirit of God at work in us. For "no one can say, 'Jesus is Lord,' except by the Holy Spirit" (1 Cor. 12:3).

WHAT DO PAUL'S INSTRUCTIONS MEAN FOR US TODAY?

How does this gospel—the unbelievable, life-transforming, history-shaping good news declared by Paul—affect our lives today? As we close this first chapter, we pause to reflect on the practical implications of Paul's instructions. This opportunity for reflection is not intended to prescribe specifically what we need to do or how we need to change in light of the truths declared by Paul. Instead, these few questions can encourage us to come before God and seek his guidance on how to respond to the truths taught by Paul.

1. Why should God let us into heaven?

2. What would be our eternal destiny if God gave us what we deserved rather than the forgiveness we can have through Christ?

3. Can we be saved by following rules and performing rituals? Why not?

4. What is the significance of the fact that salvation is a gift to be received in faith rather than something to be earned through good works? What is the significance of this fact to our daily walk as Christians?

5. What is the significance of the fact that the gospel is centered on Christ and what he did, rather than on us and our efforts? How should this reality affect our daily walk as Christians?

6. What does it mean to accept the gospel in faith? At an intellectual level, how do we accept the gospel? How does receiving the gospel in faith go beyond intellectual acceptance?

7. Can we fully understand the mystery and miracle of the gospel? Why not?

8. If we cannot be saved by our own good works, what is the role of good works in a Christian's life (which will be discussed at length in Part II of our study)?

9. What is your relationship with Christ? Is he both your Lord and Savior?

10. How should we live differently in light of the gospel?

CHAPTER 2

The Threats of Addition and Subtraction

Once we accept the gospel message in faith, one of the biggest challenges is to remain faithful to it. Some receive the gospel with enthusiasm, but over time seem to forget the pure and simple gospel preached by Paul. Pride can tempt us to turn our focus away from Christ and onto ourselves. The problem, of course, is that we can't save ourselves. Thus, in his letters, Paul calls us back again and again to the gospel. He also sternly warns about the threats that come from adding to or subtracting from the pure and simple gospel of Jesus Christ.

> ## HOW IMPORTANT IS IT FOR US TO REMAIN FAITHFUL TO THE GOSPEL?

The purity of the gospel must be vigorously protected. When he insists on adherence to the essentials of the gospel, Paul speaks in extremely harsh terms—indeed, more harshly than on any other matter he addresses. Consider the judgment pronounced by Paul in Galatians 1:8–9 on anyone who would distort the gospel:

> But even if we or an angel from heaven should preach a gospel other than the one we preached to you, let them be under God's curse! As we have already said, so now I say again: If anybody is preaching to you a gospel other than what you accepted, let them be under God's curse!

Reinforcing the seriousness of this matter, other translations of the Bible state the judgment in this passage on those who distort the gospel as "let him be eternally condemned!" (NIV 1984 version) and "let him be accursed" (King James Version, Revised Standard Version, and English Standard Version).

In Galatians and other letters, Paul confronted a distortion of the gospel that would have added a requirement that believers follow a set of legal rules and rituals—most prominently, compliance with the Old Testament law—as a condition for salvation. He warns that the people promoting this position are "trying to pervert the gospel of Christ" (Gal. 1:7). Focusing on their misguided insistence that believers undergo the Old Testament ritual of circumcision, Paul warns: "Watch out for those dogs, those evildoers, those mutilators of the flesh" (Phil. 3:2). In especially graphic terms, Paul exclaims: "I wish they would go the whole way and emasculate themselves!" (Gal. 5:12).

Although there are certainly many issues about which Christians can disagree while remaining within the faith (as further discussed in chapter 3 of our study), Paul is adamant that distortions to the essentials of the gospel cannot be tolerated. The very message of salvation is at stake.

WHAT IS AN EXAMPLE OF AN "ADDITION" TO THE GOSPEL?

Paul does not use a long list of theological terms to describe heresies that threaten the gospel. Labels like gnosticism, docetism, monarchianism, arianism, and antitrinitarianism have been used by theologians through the centuries to identify heresies. In contrast, Paul speaks in much simpler terms about remaining faithful to the gospel in the face of two types of threats: (1) additions to the essentials of the gospel, and (2) subtractions from the gospel.

An example of the threat of addition confronted by Paul and the other apostles was the false teaching that "unless you are circumcised, according to the custom taught by Moses, you cannot be saved" (Acts 15:1), and that "the Gentiles must be circumcised and required to keep the law of Moses" (Acts 15:5). This attempt to add legalistic requirements to the gospel was firmly rejected by the apostles at the Council in Jerusalem as recorded in Acts 15:1–29.

This same rejection of legalism as the basis for salvation can be found in Paul's letters. In Galatians 3:1–5, Paul states:

> You foolish Galatians! Who has bewitched you? Before your very eyes Jesus Christ was clearly portrayed as crucified. I would like to learn just one thing from you: Did you receive the Spirit by the works of the law, or by believing what you heard? Are you so foolish? After beginning by means of the Spirit, are you now trying to finish by means of the flesh? Have you experienced so much in vain—if it really was in vain? So again I ask, does God give you his Spirit and work miracles among you by the works of the law, or by your believing what you heard?

Legalism can never be the basis for salvation as Paul emphasizes in Romans 3:19–31, Romans 4:1–25, 2 Corinthians 3:6–16, Galatians 3:6–25, Galatians 6:13–16 and Philippians 3:2–11. In fact, legalism is a rejection of the gospel message that Christ's death and resurrection—not our works—are the exclusive grounds for our salvation.

Today, Christians generally understand that we are not subject to the Old Testament system of rules and rituals, such as circumcision. We nevertheless are often tempted to fall back to a legalistic or ritualistic approach toward salvation. We may rely, for example, on church attendance or programs, which may be very good but cannot save us from our sins.

While there can be a proper place for rules and rituals in a Christian's life, Paul warns in Colossians 2:20–22 that:

> Since you died with Christ to the elemental spiritual forces of this world, why, as though you still belonged to the world, do you submit to its rules: "Do not handle! Do not taste! Do not touch!"? These rules, which have to do with things that are all destined to perish with use, are based on merely human commands and teachings.

In the verses immediately preceding this passage, Paul warns against anyone who would "judge you by what you eat or drink, or with regard to a religious festival, a New Moon celebration or a Sabbath day" (Col. 2:16). This same false appearance of righteousness based on rules and rituals threatens today to distract us from the essentials of the gospel. Paul is clear that any addition to the gospel must be rejected.

WHAT IS AN EXAMPLE OF A "SUBTRACTION" FROM THE GOSPEL?

Perhaps the most common threat of subtraction comes from those who claim to be Christians, but when they use the name of "Jesus," they mean someone other than the Jesus of the gospel. Paul warns about anyone who "preaches a Jesus other than the Jesus we preached" (2 Cor. 11:4). Some simply acknowledge that Jesus was a great teacher, a miracle worker, or even a special person who possessed a spark of God. All of these descriptions miss the mark of the Jesus preached by Paul. Jesus does not simply point the way like a great teacher or bring life and health like a healer. Much more than that, Jesus declares about himself: "I am the way and the truth and the life" (John 14:6). As we discussed in chapter 1, Paul clearly identifies the Jesus of the gospel as the one in whom "all the fullness of the Deity lives in bodily form" (Col. 2:9). He is God made flesh who lived a sinless life, who accepted the punishment for our sins, and who then conquered death through his resurrection. No other "Jesus" can save us.

Another threat of subtraction identified by Paul comes from those who deny that Christ actually died on the cross for our sins or rose from the grave. In 1 Corinthians 15:12–58 (which is also discussed in chapter 1 of our study), Paul confronts a false teaching that denied the resurrection. Emphasizing this essential element of the gospel, Paul explains that "if Christ has not been raised, our preaching is useless and so is your faith" (1 Cor. 15:14). "And if Christ has not been raised, your faith is futile; you are still in your sins" (1 Cor. 15:17). This subtraction takes away an essential element of the gospel message without which we have no hope of eternal life.

WHO POSES THESE THREATS TO THE GOSPEL?

Rather than pointing to outsiders making overt threats to the Christian faith, Paul identifies the primary source of threats to the gospel as those who claim to be Christians. He therefore urges that we keep up our guards when listening to "Christian" teachers. In Galatians 2:4, Paul reports that "some false believers had infiltrated our ranks to spy on the freedom we have in Christ Jesus and to make us slaves." In 2 Corinthians 11:13, he warns of "false apostles, deceitful workers, masquerading as apostles of Christ." We need to be on guard because: "Satan himself masquerades as an angel of light. It is not surprising, then, if his servants also masquerade as servants of righteousness" (2 Cor. 11:14–15).

These false teachers "want to impress people" (Gal. 6:12) with "false humility" (Col. 2:18) and "smooth talk" (Rom. 16:18). But they "are not serving our Lord Christ, but their own appetites" (Rom. 16:18) and have as their true motive "to avoid being persecuted for the cross of Christ" (Gal. 6:12). As to those who would "deceive you with empty words," Paul instructs "do not be partners with them" (Eph. 5:6–7). We are to "watch out" for false teachers and "keep away from them" (Rom. 16:17).

Today, we need to exercise care when listening to religious teachers on the radio, TV or internet. Some are good, some bad. Because we lack a personal firsthand connection with these teachers, it is easy to be drawn in by their polished media presentations. And because they often have no real accountability—other than to ratings and marketing results—there can be a real risk of their wandering from the gospel. We are charged by Paul to exercise discernment by measuring their teaching by the standards of the gospel as declared in the Bible. Don't assume that a person is reliable simply because he or she is likable or a polished speaker.

Paul emphasizes the content of a person's message, rather than the person's appearance, as of greatest importance. A threat to the gospel may come from someone who is extremely likeable and seems to fit right in with us. Conversely, in Philippians 1:15–18, Paul describes preachers who were on poor terms with him on a personal level, even noting that they were trying to "stir up trouble for me while I am in chains" (v. 17). Yet, when discussing their ministry, he concludes in Philippians 1:18 by stating:

> But what does it matter? The important thing is that in every way, whether from false motives or true, Christ is preached. And because of this I rejoice. Yes, and I will continue to rejoice.

In the context of our churches or other communities of believers, Paul's clear instruction is to respect and honor teachers and other leaders. "Now we ask you, brothers and sisters, to acknowledge those who work hard among you, who care for you in the Lord and who admonish you. Hold them in the highest regard in love because of their work" (1 Thess. 5:12–13). As they faithfully preach the gospel, we have a duty to respect and honor them even if we do not happen to like them. But if they add to or subtract from the gospel, we ultimately must reject their message no matter how much we happen to like them.

WHY ISN'T THE CONTENT OF THE GOSPEL OPEN FOR DEBATE?

If the gospel were the product of human reasoning or tradition, it might be susceptible to alteration based on intellectual debate or human ingenuity. However, in Galatians 1:11–12, Paul declares: "I want you to know, brothers and sisters, that the gospel I preached is not of human origin. I did not receive it from any man, nor was I taught it; rather, I received it by revelation from Jesus Christ." After referring to "the mystery made known to me by revelation" (Eph. 3:3), he continues:

> In reading this, then, you will be able to understand my insight

into the mystery of Christ, which was not made known to people in other generations as it has now been revealed by the Spirit to God's holy apostles and prophets. This mystery is that through the gospel the Gentiles are heirs together with Israel, members together of one body, and sharers together in the promise in Christ Jesus. (Eph. 3:4–6)

If we humans made up a salvation story, we might tell about people who overcame their difficulties through hard work and determination. Or our salvation story might involve a superhero who defeats the oppressor and frees the innocent victims. This is the stuff of movies and novels. In contrast, the gospel of Jesus Christ involves a story of sinners who deserve condemnation. Would we humans make up a story where we are cast in such an embarrassing role? Moreover, unlike a typical man-made tale, the "hero" in the gospel story suffers a humiliating death in our place. We don't earn or deserve salvation; we receive it as a gift by our Savior's ultimate sacrifice.

While the gospel is not something we would make up, it nevertheless resonates in our souls with its elegant simplicity. The simplicity of the gospel—as well as its contrast to man-made religion—testifies to its origin with God rather than man.

Yet this gospel message can be difficult for a prideful person to accept. In our pride, we do not want to believe either that we are sinners without excuse before God, or that we can be saved only by receiving a gift we do not deserve. The gospel message thus may seem foolish from a purely human perspective. In 1 Corinthians 1:18–25, Paul observed:

For the message of the cross is foolishness to those who are perishing, but to us who are being saved it is the power of God. For it is written: "I will destroy the wisdom of the wise; the intelligence of the intelligent I will frustrate." Where is the wise person? Where is the teacher of the law? Where is the philosopher of this age? Has not God made foolish the wisdom of the world? For since in the wisdom of God the world through its wisdom did not know him, God was pleased through the foolishness of what was preached to save those who believe. Jews demand signs and Greeks look for wisdom, but we preach Christ crucified: a stumbling block to Jews and foolishness to Gentiles, but to those whom God has called, both Jews and Greeks, Christ the power of God and the wisdom of God. For the foolishness of God is wiser than human wisdom, and the weakness of God is stronger than human strength.

Paul elaborates on this point in 1 Corinthians 2:4–5 by declaring: "My message and my preaching were not with wise and persuasive words, but with a demonstration of the Spirit's power, so that your faith might not rest on human wisdom, but on God's power." He explains that since God's wisdom is much deeper and truer than human wisdom, we need to be instructed by the Spirit to understand and accept it. "The person without the Spirit does not accept the things that come from the Spirit of God but considers them foolishness, and cannot understand them because they are discerned only through the Spirit" (1 Cor. 2:14).

We are called to accept the gospel "not as a human word, but as it actually is, the word of God, which is indeed at work in you who believe" (1 Thess. 2:13). By itself, human reasoning cannot bring us to the gospel. While the gospel message is thoroughly reasonable when properly understood, it is only by God's revelation through the Holy Spirit that we can come to this proper understanding. The gospel is "the mystery hidden for long ages past, but now revealed and made known through the prophetic writings by the command of the eternal God, so that all Gentiles might come to the obedience that comes from faith—to the only wise God be glory forever through Jesus Christ! Amen" (Rom. 16:25–27).

We can thank God that the content of the gospel is not open to debate. Since the gospel was written by God, not by us, we can trust it perfectly for salvation.

WHAT DO PAUL'S INSTRUCTIONS MEAN FOR US TODAY?

Pause and reflect on Paul's instructions about threats to the gospel. Use the following questions to consider carefully how his instructions should touch and transform your heart, mind and life:

1. How are we tempted at times to fall back into a religious system based on rules and rituals rather than on our relationship with Jesus Christ as Lord and Savior?

2. Why are we sometimes inclined to add requirements to the gospel? How does our pride and desire to "earn" salvation interfere with our willingness to accept the gospel message?

3. What threats of addition to and subtraction from the gospel do we see today?

4. How can we guard against those threats?

5. How can regular Bible study help us guard against threats to the gospel?

6. What is the importance of attending a church that faithfully teaches God's Word?

7. When we listen to Christian teachers on TV or radio, do we exercise care in considering whether they are faithful to the gospel message (as well as the truths of Scripture in general)?

8. How should we respond when we hear teaching that appears contrary to the gospel message?

9. How can the gospel build unity among believers? How is unity on the essentials of the gospel compatible with liberty on nonessentials?

10. How should we live differently in light of the threats to the gospel?

CHAPTER 3

Freedom in Christ

Christians are united in and through the gospel centered on the person of Jesus Christ, his death on the cross for our sins, and his resurrection from the dead. Yet, while united by these central truths, our religious practices and views on secondary issues may differ significantly from those of other believers. This reality is apparent when believers from different denominations and different cultures come together to share our common faith. During Bible studies in my church, workplace and home, I have been struck by how Christians can be united in the gospel, yet so easily divided when we focus on religious practices and secondary issues. In this chapter, we will explore Paul's instructions on how to exercise our freedom in Christ in a manner that honors God, expresses our personal convictions, and respects the differing views held by other believers.

WHAT TYPES OF DIFFERENCES EXISTED AMONG EARLY CHRISTIANS?

Early Christians, like believers today, engaged in a variety of different practices that reflected their personal, cultural and religious backgrounds. Some treated certain days as sacred while others considered every day alike (Rom. 14:5). Some did not eat certain foods while others ate everything (Rom. 14:2). Some even went into the marketplace and bought food that had been sacrificed to pagan idols (1 Cor. 8:4), which may have been sold at a discount. In short, they, like us, had a wide range of practices on issues not tied directly to the essentials of the gospel.

Paul did not try to force compliance with a single set of religious views or practices on secondary issues. Instead, Paul instructs: "The one who eats everything must not treat with contempt the one who does not, and the one who does not eat everything must not judge the one who does, for God has accepted them" (Rom. 14:3). He provides similar instructions regarding those with differing views on whether some days are more sacred than other days (Rom. 14:5–8). Further, as discussed later in this chapter, Paul even allows for differing practices on what must have been the very sensitive issue of eating food sacrificed to idols.

Paul teaches freedom and tolerance on secondary matters even when another believer's view is clearly mistaken. On the issue of dietary practices, Paul states plainly: "I am convinced, being fully persuaded in the Lord Jesus, that nothing is unclean in itself" (Rom. 14:14). Further, when discussing believers who restrict their diet on religious grounds, Paul states: "One person's faith allows them to eat anything, but another, whose faith is weak, eats only vegetables" (Rom. 14:2). He nevertheless instructs that we should not look down on believers who restrict their diets for religious purposes (Rom. 14:3). In short, we should not try to impose our views on secondary matters on other believers—even if we are fully persuaded of the rightness of our views.

There is a great danger when we elevate the importance of our views on secondary matters to the point of treating those with differing views as outside the faith. In 1 Timothy 4:1–3, Paul addresses a situation where some teachers apparently required people to adopt practices on secondary matters as a condition to being considered true believers. "They forbid people to marry and order them to abstain from certain foods, which God created to be received with thanksgiving by those who believe and know the truth" (1 Tim. 4:3). Significantly, Paul speaks about these false teachers who "abandon the faith and follow deceiving spirits and things taught by demons" (1 Tim. 4:1).

Whatever our personal convictions on secondary matters, we have no right to demand that others comply with those convictions or to limit their freedom in how they seek to honor God within the context of the gospel.

HOW SHOULD WE DECIDE ON PERSONAL PRACTICES
AND VIEWS ON SECONDARY ISSUES?

Paul emphasizes our tremendous freedom in Christ. "Now the Lord is the Spirit, and where the Spirit of the Lord is, there is freedom" (2 Cor. 3:17). "It is for freedom that Christ has set us free. Stand firm, then, and do not let yourselves be burdened by a yoke of slavery" (Gal. 5:1). Thus, rather than prescribing a detailed set of personal practices or imposing rigid views on secondary issues, Paul calls us to exercise freedom in Christ.

Paul also provides practical instructions on how best to exercise this freedom. First, we should consider prayerfully whether, through a particular practice, we are expressing thanks to God and seeking to glorify him. In 1 Corinthians 10:31, Paul writes: "So whether you eat or drink or whatever you do, do it all for the glory of God." Similarly, in Romans 14:6, Paul observes: "Whoever regards one day as special does so to the Lord. Whoever eats meat does so to the Lord, for they give thanks to God; and whoever abstains does so to the Lord and gives thanks to God." If we are not giving thanks and seeking to glorify God in and through a particular personal practice, then it probably is not the right one to adopt.

Second, we should consider thoughtfully and prayerfully how our views and practices reflect our faith in Christ. When discussing two individuals with fundamentally different views about whether some days are more sacred than others, Paul declares: "Each of them should be fully convinced in their own mind" (Rom. 14:5). Do not engage in practices that you believe to be improper. "If anyone regards something as unclean, then for that person it is unclean" (Rom. 14:14). This is because "everything that does not come from faith is sin" (Rom. 14:23).

Third, Paul cautions against adopting views and practices simply because others happen to hold them. "For why is my freedom being judged by another's conscience?" (1 Cor. 10:29). "Therefore do not let anyone judge you by what you eat or drink, or with regard to a religious festival, a New Moon celebration or a Sabbath day" (Col. 2:16). Thus, while Paul addresses the need to be *sensitive* to the practices of other believers (as discussed in the following section), he emphasizes that this sensitivity does not mean that you are *bound* by the religious practices or personal convictions of others. When discussing his willingness to accommodate others, he begins by stating: "I am free and belong to no one" (1 Cor. 9:19).

While some might want detailed direction on every point of religious practice or every secondary issue, Paul does not provide it for good reason—because it would distract from the central truths of the gospel and deprive us of the freedom that we have in Christ. Indeed, an attempt to create such all-encompassing rules could lead to a legalistic system like the one from which Christ freed us.

Paul instead emphasizes the importance of maintaining a strong relationship with Christ. We cannot have a real relationship with a set of rules or rituals. Rather, Christ has invited us into a personal relationship with God. Paul therefore calls us to adopt practices based on prayerful consideration and personal convictions that flow from that all-important relationship.

HOW SHOULD WE DEAL WITH OTHERS WHO HAVE DIFFERENT PERSONAL PRACTICES AND CONVICTIONS ON SECONDARY ISSUES?

Paul identifies two very practical principles for dealing with differences between believers on secondary issues. First, we should not be judgmental toward fellow believers. When discussing different dietary practices among Christians, Paul asks in Romans 14:4: "Who are you to judge someone else's servant? To their own master, servants stand or fall. And they will stand, for the Lord is able to make them stand." He continues in Romans 14:13–15 by explaining:

> Therefore let us stop passing judgment on one another. Instead, make up your mind not to put any stumbling block or obstacle in the way of a brother or sister. I am convinced, being fully persuaded in the Lord Jesus, that nothing is unclean in itself. But if

anyone regards something as unclean, then for that person it is unclean. If your brother or sister is distressed because of what you eat, you are no longer acting in love. Do not by your eating destroy someone for whom Christ died.

A second principle repeatedly identified by Paul is the need to put others first. After explaining that our purpose is "not to please ourselves," he instructs: "Each of us should please our neighbors for their good, to build them up" (Rom. 15:1–2). "No one should seek their own good, but the good of others" (1 Cor. 10:24). "Let us therefore make every effort to do what leads to peace and to mutual edification" (Rom. 14:19). "Accept one another, then, just as Christ accepted you, in order to bring praise to God" (Rom. 15:7). When we put others first, what seemed to be serious differences on secondary issues can begin to lose some significance.

In 1 Corinthians 9:19–23, Paul illustrates how he applied these principles in his own life:

Though I am free and belong to no one, I have made myself a slave to everyone, to win as many as possible. To the Jews I became like a Jew, to win the Jews. To those under the law I became like one under the law (though I myself am not under the law), so as to win those under the law. To those not having the law I became like one not having the law (though I am not free from God's law but am under Christ's law), so as to win those not having the law. To the weak I became weak, to win the weak. I have become all things to all people so that by all possible means I might save some. I do all this for the sake of the gospel, that I may share in its blessings.

Paul's instructions in this area may be reminiscent of what you may have learned as a child in Sunday school: A Christian spells J-O-Y by putting Jesus first, then Others, and finally Yourself. In Paul's words:

So whether you eat or drink or whatever you do, do it for the glory of God. Do not cause anyone to stumble, whether Jews, Greeks or the church of God—even as I try to please everyone in every way. For I am not seeking my own good but the good of many, so that they may be saved. (1 Cor. 10:31–33)

WHAT SHOULD WE DO WHEN CONFRONTED WITH POTENTIALLY DIVISIVE DIFFERENCES OF OPINION?

In 1 Corinthians 8 and 10, Paul confronts the very sensitive issue of whether Christians should eat meat sacrificed to idols. We too confront emotion-filled differences among believers—in the areas of politics, environmental stewardship, drinking, dancing, and a host of other issues. Although many early Christians apparently found repugnant the practice of eating food sacrificed to a pagan idol, Paul nevertheless indicates in 1 Corinthians 8:1–6 that a believer is free to eat meat from any source. Yet he also cautions in verse 9 of that same chapter: "Be careful, however, that the exercise of your rights does not become a stumbling block to the weak."

Illustrating what it means in practice to put others first and not be judgmental, Paul provides guidance on specific situations related to food sacrificed to idols:

- After explaining that "we know that 'An idol is nothing at all in the world' and that 'There is no God but one'" (1 Cor. 8:4), Paul nevertheless observes: "Some people are still so accustomed to idols that when they eat sacrificial food they think of it as having been sacrificed to a god, and since their conscience is weak, it is defiled" (1 Cor. 8:7). Paul therefore would not eat meat sacrificed to idols in the presence of these individuals because it could undermine their faith. "When you sin against them in this way and wound their weak conscience, you sin against Christ. Therefore, if what I eat causes my brother or sister to fall into sin, I will never eat meat again, so that I will not cause them to fall" (1 Cor. 8:12–13).

- Paul also instructs: "If an unbeliever invites you to a meal and you want to go, eat whatever is put before you without raising questions of conscience" (1 Cor. 10:27). But if your host makes a point of saying that the meat had been sacrificed to an idol—perhaps to test the sincerity of your faith in Christ—then don't eat it because apparently it might cause the unbeliever to conclude that you do not take your faith seriously. (1 Cor. 10:28–30)

We all can think of issues that, within our churches or other communities of believers, have the potential to cause controversy and division. Christians have a wide range of views on many political, social and cultural matters. We often choose to raise our families differently and engage in differing lifestyles. While there are some issues on which the Bible directs us to draw distinct lines (including the essentials of the gospel as discussed in chapter 2 and sinful conduct by believers that violate God's clear commands as discussed later in this chapter), there are gray areas—such as what Paul calls "disputable matters" (Rom. 14:1)—where you may have strongly held and emotional views that differ from those held by other believers with equal vigor.

We need discernment and discretion in these situations. While the best course of action may vary depending on specific facts, Paul's instructions on the issue of eating food sacrificed to idols—which seems as potentially controversial as almost any secondary issue that we might confront today—provide a model for sensitivity that we should consider when addressing potentially divisive issues. We can have strongly held views on an issue without forcing them on others. In short, Paul counsels against unnecessary confrontation on secondary issues.

HOW SHOULD WE EXERCISE OUR FREEDOM WITHIN OUR LOCAL CHURCHES?

If we all simply did our own thing when we gather with other believers—each engaging in a preferred practice without appropriate sensitivity to others—there would be disorder and destructive results. Imagine a meeting where some are singing loudly while others try to listen to a teaching, or where people are talking over each other so no one can understand what is being said.

Paul confronted this type of situation in 1 Corinthians 14:26–40. Emphasizing the need for order during church meetings, he explains that "God is not a God of disorder but of peace" (v. 33) and "everything should be done in a fitting and orderly way" (v. 40). In light of the divisions and disorder within the Corinthian church (as apparent from several passages including 1 Cor. 3:3–9; 6:1–7; 11:17–22), Paul provides very specific guidance to the Corinthian believers—much more specific than found in his other letters—on their worship practices. For example, he identifies an appropriate number of individuals who should speak in tongues (1 Cor. 14:27) and prophesy (1 Cor. 14:29) when the church meets.

It is in this context that he also provides instructions—which may have layers of meaning beyond the subject of this chapter—on practices related to women wearing head coverings (1 Cor. 11:2–16) and speaking in church (1 Cor. 14:34–38). Paul explains this guidance in part by pointing to the practices followed generally in the churches of his day. He concludes his discussion of head covering by stating: "If anyone wants to be contentious about this, we have no other practice—nor do the churches of God" (1 Cor. 11:16). He makes a similar reference in 1 Corinthians 14:33, when explaining a practice as one followed "in all the congregations of the Lord's people."

The point here is that, for the sake of unity and decorum, we need to set aside some of our personal preferences when we come together as a group of believers. This principle, which would apply to the orderly operation of any group, is necessary to our harmonious worship as we gather together as a church. We have freedom in Christ, certainly, but that same Christ calls us to unity and order when we come together.

IS FREEDOM IN CHRIST AN EXCUSE FOR SIN?

Absolutely not. In Galatians 5:13, Paul directs: "You, my brothers and sisters, were called to be free. But do not use your freedom to indulge the flesh; rather, serve one another humbly in love." In 1 Corinthians 10:23, he corrects those who would assert that "I have the right to do anything," by explaining that "not everything is beneficial" and "not everything is constructive."

We have misunderstood the gospel if we view our freedom in Christ as a license to sin. In Romans 6:1–2, Paul asks rhetorically: "What shall we say, then? Shall we go on sinning so that grace may increase? By no means! We are those who have died to sin; how can we live in it any longer?" Regarding anyone who would say, "Let us do evil that good may result," Paul states emphatically: "Their condemnation is just" (Rom. 3:8).

Freedom in Christ does not mean tolerance of sin, either in our personal lives or in the life of the church. As discussed further in chapter 10 of this book, Paul confronts the open sexual sin of a church member in 1 Corinthians 5:11, where he instructs: "But now I am writing you that you must not associate with anyone who claims to be a brother or sister but is sexually immoral or greedy, an idolater or a slanderer, a drunkard or a swindler. Do not even eat with such people." Similarly, in 2 Thessalonians 3:14, he instructs: "Take special note of anyone who does not obey our instruction in this letter. Do not associate with him, in order that he may feel ashamed."

Significantly, by not associating with someone claiming to be a Christian but who is engaged in open and unrepentant sin, Paul makes clear that this action is intended to lead to that individual's repentance and restoration. In 2 Corinthians 2:6–7, Paul specifically addresses this need for restoration after repentance (perhaps of the same individual identified in 1 Corinthians 5 noted above) by explaining: "The punishment inflicted on him by the majority is sufficient. Now instead, you ought to forgive and comfort him, so that he will not be overwhelmed by excessive sorrow." Similarly, when giving direction on dealing with a disobedient church member, Paul explains the need for discipline but also states: "Yet do not regard them as an enemy, but warn them as you would a fellow believer" (2 Thess. 3:15).

Sin is not a "disputable matter" (Rom. 14:1) where we can claim freedom in Christ as an excuse for ignoring God's commands. When God speaks clearly, we need to obey. While we have tremendous freedom in Christ, and many of the differing practices among Christians have their basis in Christian liberty, our freedom is not a license for sin. May God give use the discernment to recognize and root out sin, as well as the wisdom to differentiate between sin and disputable secondary matters.

Although a champion of freedom in Christ, Paul nevertheless identifies proper limitations on our exercise of this freedom. Most importantly, the gospel message of salvation provides the foundation for this freedom and, as discussed in chapter 2, we certainly are not free to add to or subtract from the gospel. Moreover, as discussed in this chapter, Paul instructs that we should not use our freedom in Christ in a manner that (1) causes others to stumble in their faith, (2) brings disorder to the church, or (3) seeks to excuse sinful conduct. We should instead use our freedom to build up—not tear down—other believers, the church, and our own spiritual condition.

WHAT DO PAUL'S INSTRUCTIONS MEAN FOR US TODAY?

Pause and reflect on Paul's instructions on our freedom in Christ. Use the following questions to consider carefully how his instructions should touch and transform your heart, mind, and life:

1. How are we tempted to fall back into the bondage of sin or man-made religion?
2. Are we using or abusing our freedom in Christ? Do we use it as an excuse for sin?
3. Do we use our freedom to build up or tear down others? Do we

use our freedom to do what we want or what God wants for us?

4. Do we put others ahead of ourselves? Are we critical and judgmental of others on nonessential matters?

5. How can we use our freedom in Christ to build bridges to others (both unbelievers and believers)?

6. What practices and patterns of behavior have we adopted based on the freedom that we have in Christ?

7. How often do we express thanks to God and seek to glorify him in our practices and patterns of behavior? How can we better do so in the future?

8. Have we carefully and prayerfully thought through our religious practices? Or are they simply a matter of routine?

9. How can we show respect and love for other believers with different practices?

10. How should we live differently in light of the freedom we have in Christ?

CHAPTER 4

The Standard of Scripture

The written Word of God—the Bible—leads us to knowledge of the living Word of God, Jesus Christ (John 1:1–14). Paul identifies a tight connection between the Bible and the gospel. As explained by Paul, the Old Testament pointed to and laid the foundation for the gospel message. The New Testament states this gospel in plain and unambiguous terms. What we believe as Christians is based on what is said in the Bible. Therefore, as believers, we look to the Bible for direction on matters of faith and practice.

> ## HOW DOES SCRIPTURE PROVIDE THE FOUNDATION FOR UNDERSTANDING THE GOSPEL MESSAGE OF SALVATION?

When declaring the essential elements of the gospel in 1 Corinthians 15:3–4, Paul ties the message of salvation directly to the Old Testament Scriptures: "For what I received I passed on to you as of first importance: that Christ died for our sins *according to the Scriptures*, that he was buried, that he was raised on the third day *according to the Scriptures*." Similarly, when put on trial for preaching the gospel, Paul explained: "I am saying nothing beyond what the prophets and Moses said would happen—that the Messiah would suffer and, as the first to rise from the dead, would bring the message of light to his own people and to the Gentiles" (Acts 26:22–23). "For everything that was written in the past was written to teach us, so that through the endurance taught in the Scriptures and the encouragement they provide we might have hope" (Rom. 15:4).

Paul speaks of "the gospel he [God] promised beforehand through his prophets in the Holy Scriptures regarding his Son, who as to his earthly life was a descendant of David, and who through the Spirit of holiness was appointed the Son of God in power by his resurrection from the dead: Jesus Christ our Lord" (Rom. 1:2–4). The Old Testament thus laid the foundation for God's revelation in Christ Jesus that salvation is available to all people. "Scripture foresaw that God would justify the Gentiles by faith, and announced the gospel in advance to Abraham" (Gal. 3:8).

Not only does the gospel have its roots in the Old Testament, but also its fulfillment is in history yet to be written. When discussing Christ's future return and the following judgment of all people, Paul explains that: "This will take place on the day when God judges people's secrets through Jesus Christ, as my gospel declares" (Rom. 2:16).

He further speaks in Colossians 1:23 of "the hope held out in the gospel." The gospel of Jesus Christ's death and resurrection is the central event in all of history—with its roots in the Old Testament prophets and its fulfillment in God's judgment yet to come.

WERE PAUL'S LETTERS RECOGNIZED AS SCRIPTURE DURING HIS LIFETIME?

The Apostle Peter specifically identified Paul's letters as Scripture. In 2 Peter 3:15–16, Peter explains that "Paul also wrote you with the wisdom that God gave him," that "he writes the same way in all his letters," and that:

> His letters contain some things that are hard to understand, which ignorant and unstable people distort, as they do *the other Scriptures*, to their own destruction.

Moreover, the Lord himself declared Paul's authority as "my chosen instrument to proclaim my name to the Gentiles and their kings and to the people of Israel" (Acts 9:15). Paul's own actions and words further establish his credentials as God's spokesperson. He testifies regarding "the gospel I preached" that "I received it by revelation from Jesus Christ" (Gal. 1:11–12). "I will not venture to speak of anything except what

Christ has accomplished through me in leading Gentiles to obey God by what I have said and done—by the power of signs and wonders, through the power of the Spirit of God" (Rom. 15:18–19). Regarding his ministry in Corinth, he explained: "I persevered in demonstrating the marks of a true apostle, including signs, wonders and miracles" (2 Cor. 12:12). Paul thus can state with authority that: "What you heard from me, keep as the pattern of sound teaching, with faith and love in Christ Jesus" (2 Tim. 1:13). "And the things you have heard me say in the presence of many witnesses entrust to reliable people who will also be qualified to teach others" (2 Tim. 2:2).

There is a common misperception that the books comprising the New Testament, including Paul's letters, which constitute thirteen of the New Testament's twenty-seven books, were not recognized as Scripture until centuries after the fact. In reality, the biblical text itself recognizes Paul's letters as Scripture.

WHAT DOES PAUL TEACH ABOUT THE OLD TESTAMENT?

Dozens of Old Testament prophecies were fulfilled by Christ's life, death, and resurrection. While there are many helpful studies of these prophecies, they are not a focus of Paul's letters—perhaps because he was writing to believers who did not need to be persuaded that Christ was the promised Messiah.

However, Paul does discuss at considerable length the question of whether the gospel message was a break from or a continuation of the Old Testament law. This issue had great practical relevance to the recipients of his letters, many of whom were Jews who recently had put their faith in Jesus Christ as the Messiah. These new believers wondered if the Old Testament law was now moot, or if it still applied to them as followers of the risen Christ. This issue remains relevant for us today because all Scripture, including the Old Testament, is intended for our instruction. While our study will not attempt to discuss all Paul has to say about the Old Testament law, we will consider his substantial instruction on how we, as Christians, should understand the Old Testament.

Emphasizing continuity with the Old Testament, Paul explains in both Romans 4 and Galatians 3 that Abraham—the father of the Jewish people—is a model of a person saved by faith and not by works. He points out that, when God promised to bless Abraham and his offspring in Genesis 15, the basis for the promise was that: "Abraham believed God, and it was credited to him as righteousness" (Rom. 4:3; Gal. 3:6).

God's covenant promise could not have been based on Abraham's following the law since God did not give the law to Moses until more than 400 years later (Gal. 3:17). Nor was this covenant promise based on circumcision, since God made it before Abraham was circumcised (Rom. 4:9–12). Instead of the law or other legalistic requirement, "the promise comes by faith, so that it may be by grace and may be guaranteed to all Abraham's offspring" (Rom. 4:16). Abraham is thus "the father of all who believe" (Rom. 4:11). "It is the children of the promise who are regarded as Abraham's offspring" (Rom. 9:8).

Given that faith has *always* been the basis for people being declared righteous by God, we might reasonably ask why God established the law in the Old Testament in the first place. A starting point for answering this question is that before the Old Testament law was given, people were sinning and needed to be told the difference between right and wrong. As Paul explains: "I would not have known what sin was had it not been for the law. For I would not have known what coveting really was if the law had not said, 'Do not covet'" (Rom. 7:7).

Once God gave the law to Moses, the Israelites to whom the law was read should have responded by doing what the law said. However, they continued to sin and, in fact, sinned even more. Paul explains that "sin, seizing the opportunity afforded by the commandment, produced in me every kind of coveting" (Rom. 7:8). "I found that the very commandment that was intended to bring life actually brought death" (Rom. 7:10). "Therefore no one will be declared righteous in God's sight by the works of the law; rather, through the law we became conscious of our sin" (Rom. 3:20).

As the law exposed our sinful nature, it also revealed our need for a Savior. In Paul's words:

- "Why, then, was the law given at all? It was added because of transgressions until the Seed [Christ] to whom the promise [by God to Abraham] referred had come" (Gal. 3:19).
- "So the law was our guardian until Christ came that we might be justified by faith" (Gal. 3:24).
- "The law was brought in so that the trespass might increase. But where sin increased, grace increased all the more, so that, just as sin reigned in death, so also grace might reign through righteousness to bring eternal life through Jesus Christ our Lord" (Rom. 5:20–21).

God thus used the law—and humanity's continuing violation of his law—to point out our need for a Savior. Paul likens the law to a guardian or trustee who cares for a child until the time came for the child to receive his or her inheritance (Gal. 4:1–3). "But when the set time had fully come, God sent his Son, born of a woman, born under the law, to redeem those under law, that we might receive adoption to sonship" (Gal. 4:4–5). "Now that this faith has come, we are no longer under a guardian" (Gal. 3:25).

To be clear, God's law is righteous and humanity's violation of God's law requires punishment. A central truth of the gospel is that God paid this penalty for our violations "by sending his own Son in the likeness of sinful flesh to be a sin offering. And so he condemned sin in the flesh, in order that the righteous requirement of the law might be fully met in us" (Rom. 8:3–4). Describing this penalty as a curse, Paul further explains: "Christ redeemed us from the curse of the law by becoming a curse for us, for it is written: 'Cursed is everyone who is hung on a pole'" (Gal. 3:13). Christ brought us peace "by setting aside in his flesh the law with its commandments and regulations" (Eph. 2:15).

Now that we are alive in Christ, we are dead to the law and it has no reign over us. "So, my brothers and sisters, you also died to the law through the body of Christ, that you might belong to another, to him who was raised from the dead, in order that we might bear fruit for God" (Rom. 7:4). "But now, by dying to what once bound us, we have been released from the law so that we serve in the new way of the Spirit, and not in the old way of the written code" (Rom. 7:6). Thus, "you are not under the law, but under grace" (Rom. 6:14). "For through the law I died to the law so that I might live for God" (Gal. 2:19). Paul explains that he does not have "a righteousness of my own that comes from the law, but that which is through faith in Christ—the righteousness that comes from God on the basis of faith" (Phil. 3:9).

All of this leads to the wonderful truth that "through Christ Jesus the law of the Spirit who gives life has set you free from the law of sin and death" (Rom. 8:2). "If you are led by the Spirit, you are not under the law" (Gal. 5:18). Instead, we are "ministers of a new covenant—not of the letter but of the Spirit; for the letter kills, but the Spirit gives life" (2 Cor. 3:6). Rather than the circumcision of the flesh required by the Old Testament law, we have a "circumcision of the heart, by the Spirit, not by the written code" (Rom. 2:29).

In addition to addressing the significance of the law for the Christian, Paul quotes extensively from the Old Testament and provides instruction from stories such as Jacob and Esau (Rom. 9:6–13), Sarah and Hagar (Gal. 4:21–31), and the Israelites wanderings in the desert under Moses (1 Cor. 10:1–10). "These things happened to them as examples and were written down as warnings to us, on whom the culmination of the ages has come" (1 Cor. 10:11).

Paul consistently interprets and applies these Old Testament lessons in light of Christ. Indeed, the Old Testament cannot be fully and properly understood by a Christian apart from the gospel of Christ. It is through Christ that the Old Testament takes on practical meaning for our lives today.

> ## HOW IS SCRIPTURE THE FOUNDATION FOR SOUND TEACHING AND DOCTRINE?

Emphasizing the importance of Scripture as the basis for sound teaching and doctrine, Paul refers to "the Holy Scriptures, which are able to make you wise for salvation through faith in Christ Jesus" (2 Tim. 3:15). He continues in the next two verses by declaring:

> All Scripture is God-breathed and is useful for teaching, rebuking, correcting and training in righteousness, so that the servant of God may be thoroughly equipped for every good work. (2 Tim. 3:16–17)

Scripture thus provides the standard for what we believe as Christians—matters of "teaching, rebuking, correcting and training in righteousness"—with the purpose of practical application "so that the servant of God may be thoroughly equipped for every good work."

We should not neglect the study and application of Scripture. It is not simply another book of helpful hints for happy living. It is "God-breathed." It both makes us "wise for salvation" and equips us for "every good work." We put our spiritual lives and our very souls at risk by neglecting the Scriptures.

WHAT IF WE HAVE A HARD TIME READING AND UNDERSTANDING SCRIPTURE?

We will never be able to fully understand and apply God's truth simply through study and intellectual rigor. There is, of course, an important role for Bible study. Our understanding can be aided by the use of commentaries, concordances, and other Bible study resources. Moreover, within our churches, pastors and teachers can help us work through difficult passages. Small group Bible studies, where we can share perspectives on the meaning and application of a passage, can also be of tremendous benefit to our understanding of Scripture.

However, as Paul explains in 1 Corinthians 2, we cannot gain a life-transforming understanding of the gospel except by the Holy Spirit. "These are the things God has revealed to us by his Spirit" (v. 10). "What we have received is not the spirit of the world, but the Spirit who is from God, so that we may understand what God has freely given us" (v. 12). "The person without the Spirit does not accept the things that come from the Spirit of God but considers them foolishness, and cannot understand them because they are discerned only through the Spirit" (v. 14). "The

Spirit searches all things, even the deep things of God" (v. 10).

Paul describes a "veil" covering the minds and hearts of unbelievers that obscures and distorts their understanding of Scripture. In 2 Corinthians 3:14–15, Paul refers to people whose "minds were made dull, for to this day the same veil remains when the old covenant is read" and that "even to this day when Moses is read, a veil covers their hearts." In 2 Corinthians 4:4, Paul further explains: "The god of this age [that is, the devil] has blinded the minds of unbelievers, so that they cannot see the light of the gospel that displays the glory of Christ who is the image of God." Removing this veil requires more than intellectual curiosity or effort. "Only in Christ is it taken away" (2 Cor. 3:14).

Explaining the glorious result when this veil is removed, Paul declares in 2 Corinthians 3:16–18 that:

> But whenever anyone turns to the Lord, the veil is taken away. Now the Lord is the Spirit, and where the Spirit of the Lord is, there is freedom. And we all, who with unveiled faces contemplate the Lord's glory, are being transformed into his image with ever-increasing glory, which comes from the Lord, who is the Spirit.

Paul thus suggests a progression in how we can understand and apply Scripture to our lives. On our own, our minds and hearts are dull to the truths of Scripture. "But whenever anyone turns to the Lord, the veil is taken away" (2 Cor. 3:16). Not only will the Spirit provide understanding of the Scripture, our lives will be "transformed into [the Lord's] image" as we ever increasingly reflect the Lord's glory (2 Cor. 3:18).

Scripture and the Spirit go hand in hand. The Word of God is in fact "the sword of the Spirit" (Eph. 6:17). We rely on the Spirit both to understand Scripture and to put its truths into practice.

WHAT DO PAUL'S INSTRUCTIONS MEAN FOR US TODAY?

Pause and reflect on Paul's instructions on the importance of Scripture. Use the following questions to consider carefully how his instructions should touch and transform our hearts, minds, and lives:

1. In practice, is the Bible really the standard that we use for determining what we believe?

2. How often should a believer read the Bible? How often do we read it?

3. Do we read the Bible differently from other books? In what ways is reading the Bible different?

4. What is the role of prayer and the Spirit's leading in Bible study? How do they affect our personal Bible reading?

5. What should we do when we encounter a difficult passage of Scripture? Is it possible to move forward without having all of our questions answered right now?

6. Do we apply what we learn through Bible study? Does it change how we think and live?

7. What does it mean to interpret Scripture—especially the Old Testament—in light of Christ and the gospel message of salvation?

8. What is the role of the Old Testament law and ritual for us today? How is Christianity both a continuation of and a break from the Old Testament?

9. Do we really believe that "all Scripture is God-breathed and is useful for teaching, rebuking, correcting and training in righteousness" (2 Tim. 3:16)? If so, how does our belief in its inspiration and authority affect our reading and application of Scripture?

10. How should we think and live differently in light of Paul's instruction on and approach to Scripture?

CHAPTER 5

Paul's Practical Theology

Paul's theology is not concerned with abstract propositions with little or no practical application. While some seem to treat theological discussions as exercises in intellectual curiosity on obscure points, Paul presents theological truths that help us understand and apply the gospel and live gospel-centered lives. In contrast to the divisions between Christians through the centuries due to theological differences of opinion, Paul explains how our unity should be strengthened by a proper understanding of theological issues such as baptism, communion, and Christ's return.

Paul does not attempt to address every point that you might find in a volume of systematic theology. As already discussed, his letters to the churches were written to regular Christians without any special theological training or educational credentials. Instead, when he discusses a point of theology, it has practical significance and application of the gospel to our lives today.

WHAT IS PAUL'S APPROACH TO CREEDS AND DOCTRINAL STATEMENTS?

Paul's letters do not contain detailed creeds or comprehensive statements of Christian beliefs. The closest that he comes to prescribing a confession of faith is in Romans 10:9, where he explains: "If you declare with your mouth, 'Jesus is Lord,' and believe in your heart that God raised him from the dead, you will be saved." It is noteworthy that this simple confession of faith puts the focus, once again, back on the gospel itself.

If we want to find Paul's most nuanced and sophisticated theological discussion, we need look no further than Romans 1 through 11. In those chapters, he lays the foundation for understanding the gospel of Jesus Christ and its implications for our lives today. His key points might be outlined as follows:

- We are all sinners who deserve God's wrath. None of us has satisfied God's standard of righteousness (Rom. 1:18 to 3:20).
- Although we are sinners deserving his wrath, God has made available a righteousness that comes through faith in Jesus Christ (Rom. 3:21 to 5:21).
- Once we receive this righteousness through faith, we should not continue to live in sin. We are to live victoriously as we are transformed by Christ and the Spirit (Rom. 6:1 to 8:39).
- In his sovereignty, God has established this plan for salvation that extends to the people of Israel as well as peoples from every nation (Rom. 9:1 to 11:36).

Similarly, as explained below, Paul's instructions on the theological issues of baptism and communion also bring us back to the gospel message.

WHAT INSTRUCTION DOES PAUL PROVIDE ON BAPTISM?

Rather than debating points about baptism that divide many believers today—such as the method, liturgy, or proper age for baptism—Paul focuses on its spiritual significance in the context of the gospel. In Romans 6:3–4, Paul explains:

Or don't you know that all of us who were baptized into Christ Jesus were baptized into his death? We were therefore buried with him through baptism into death in order that, just as Christ was raised from the dead through the glory of the Father, we too may live a new life.

Again emphasizing that baptism concerns identification and participation with Christ, Paul declares in Galatians 3:26–27 that: "So in Christ Jesus you are all children of God through faith, for all of you who were baptized into Christ have clothed yourselves with Christ."

Paul further explains that baptism speaks of our unity in Christ. "For we were all baptized by one Spirit so as to form one body—whether Jews or Gentiles, slave or free—and we were all given the one Spirit to drink" (1 Cor. 12:13). Paul also discusses baptism in 1 Corinthians 1:10–17 when warning against divisions between believers. Baptism should remind us of our unity in the gospel, not divide us based on differences of opinion not directly related to the gospel.

WHAT INSTRUCTION DOES PAUL PROVIDE ON COMMUNION?

When explaining the importance of communion, Paul again focuses on how it reflects our identification and participation in the gospel:

> Is not the cup of thanksgiving for which we give thanks a participation in the blood of Christ? And is not the bread that we break a participation in the body of Christ? Because there is one loaf, we, who are many, are one body, for we all share the one loaf. (1 Cor. 10:16–17)

Again, in 1 Corinthians 11:23–26, Paul declares the true meaning and purpose of communion:

> For I received from the Lord what I also passed on to you: The Lord Jesus, on the night he was betrayed, took bread, and when he had given thanks, he broke it and said, "This is my body, which is for you, do this in remembrance of me." In the same way, after supper he took the cup, saying, "This cup is the new covenant in my blood; do this, whenever you drink it, in

remembrance of me." For whenever you eat this bread and drink this cup, you proclaim the Lord's death until he comes.

Paul thus brings the discussion back to a core element of the gospel: Christ's death. Communion is a reminder of Christ's sacrifice on the cross by which our sins are forgiven.

Communion, like baptism, also speaks of our unity as Christians in and through the gospel. In 1 Corinthians 10:17, Paul explains that "we, who are many, are one body, for we all share the one loaf." He uses very similar words later in the same letter when discussing the church as the body of Christ. "Just as a body, though one, has many parts, but all of its many parts form one body, so it is with Christ" (1 Cor. 12:12). "Even so the body is not made up of one part but of many" (1 Cor. 12:14). "As it is, there are many parts, but one body" (1 Cor. 12:20). While we will discuss relationships within the church as the body of Christ further in chapter 13 of our study, the point here is that Paul's discussion of communion highlights the practical and important point of our unity in Christ.

In light of the importance of communion, Paul issues a stern warning that "whoever eats the bread or drinks the cup of the Lord in an unworthy manner will be guilty of sinning against the body and blood of the Lord" (1 Cor. 11:27). This warning was given to the church in Corinth because "when you come together, it is not the Lord's Supper you eat, for when you are eating, some of you go ahead with your own private suppers. As a result, one person remains hungry and another gets drunk" (1 Cor. 11:20–21). Rebuking them for disrespecting both the Lord and each other in this manner, Paul states: "For those who eat and drink without discerning the body of Christ eat and drink judgment on themselves. That is why many among you are weak and sick, and a number of you have fallen asleep" (1 Cor. 11:29–30). He further instructs: "Everyone ought to examine themselves before they eat of the bread and drink from the cup" (1 Cor. 11:28). "But if we were more discerning with regard to ourselves, we would not come under such judgment. Nevertheless, when we are judged in this way by the Lord, we are being disciplined so that we will not be finally condemned with the world" (1 Cor. 11:31–32).

As with baptism, Paul focuses on the spiritual and practical importance of communion rather than detailed theological distinctions. He calls us to a fuller appreciation of and unity through the gospel resulting from a proper understanding of communion.

WHEN WILL CHRIST RETURN AND WHAT WILL IT BE LIKE?

Many Christians debate the details of when Christ will return and how it will happen. For Paul, Christ's return is important not for these details but because it flows from the gospel truths of Christ's death and resurrection. When discussing Christ's return, Paul explains: "For we believe that Jesus died and rose again, and so we believe that God will bring with Jesus those who have fallen asleep in him" (1 Thess. 4:14). Paul uses the term "fallen asleep" to refer to Christians who have died.

While many people view death as an end, it is a glorious beginning for Christians because our Savior rose from the dead and thus provides assurance that we, too, will be raised. Paul instructs: "Brothers and sisters, we do not want you to be uninformed about those who sleep in death, so that you do not grieve like the rest of mankind, who have no hope" (1 Thess. 4:13). We have this hope because "the Lord himself will come down from heaven, with a loud command, with the voice of the archangel and with the trumpet call of God, and the dead in Christ will rise first. After that, we who are still alive and are left will be caught up together with them in the clouds to meet the Lord in the air. And so we will be with the Lord forever" (1 Thess. 4:16–17).

Paul also seeks to calm any concern that Christ had already returned and that we somehow missed it. "Concerning the coming of our Lord Jesus Christ and our being gathered to him, we ask you, brothers and sisters, not to become easily unsettled or alarmed by the teaching allegedly from us—whether by a prophecy or by word of mouth or by letter—asserting that the day of the Lord has already come. Don't let anyone deceive you in any way" (2 Thess. 2:1–3). Much must happen before Christ's return (2 Thess. 2:1–2), including the appearance of "the man of lawlessness" who "sets himself up in God's temple, proclaiming himself to be God" (2 Thess. 2:3–4). "The coming of the lawless one will be in accordance with how Satan works. He will use all sorts of displays of power through signs and wonders that serve the lie, and all the ways that wickedness deceives those who are perishing" (2 Thess. 2:9–10). While the details of these events may be open to reasonable debate and disagreement, the world-changing reality of Christ's return will be impossible for anyone to overlook!

And while Paul does not identify precisely when Christ will return, he does speak with certainty of both the terrible judgment and marvelous glory on that day:

> This will happen when the Lord Jesus is revealed from heaven in blazing fire with his powerful angels. He will punish those who do not know God and do not obey the gospel of our Lord Jesus. They will be punished with everlasting destruction and shut out from the presence of the Lord and from the glory of his might on the day he comes to be glorified in his holy people and to be marveled at among all those who have believed. This includes you, because you believed our testimony to you. (2 Thess. 1:7–10)

All believers "will be made alive" on the day "when he comes" (1 Cor. 15:22–23) and:

> Then the end will come, when he hands over the kingdom to God the Father after he has destroyed all dominion, authority and power. For he must reign until he has put all his enemies under his feet. The last enemy to be destroyed is death. (1 Cor. 15:24–26)

While we do not know the date when we will be raised to eternal glory, we have the assurance of that glory because we have a risen Savior with authority over death. "For through the Spirit we eagerly await by faith the righteousness for which we hope" (Gal. 5:5).

The present reality of the Spirit in our hearts is evidence of our future inheritance. God "has given us the Spirit as a deposit, guaranteeing what is to come" (2 Cor. 5:5). "He anointed us, set his seal of ownership on us, and put his Spirit in our hearts as a deposit, guaranteeing what is to come" (2 Cor. 1:21–22). "When you believed, you were marked in him with a seal, the promised Holy Spirit, who is a deposit guaranteeing our inheritance until the redemption of those who are God's possession—to the praise of his glory" (Eph. 1:13–14). "We ourselves, who have the firstfruits of the Spirit, groan inwardly as we wait eagerly for our adoption to sonship, the redemption of our bodies" (Rom. 8:23).

What about free will and predestination?

Perhaps the most hotly debated point of theology from Paul's letters to the churches is the issue of free will and predestination. Widely differing views on this subject are held by mature and thoughtful believers. Rather than attempt to resolve those differences (which is well beyond the purpose of this book—and even further beyond my ability), I will make a few observations based on Paul's letters that may help us put this issue in practical perspective.

While many characterize the issue as free will *versus* predestination, Paul seems to consider it a matter of free will *and* predestination. Indeed, we can find plenty in Paul's letters (and, indeed, in the Bible as a whole) to support both—which helps explain how apologists for one view or another can claim that the Bible supports their positions.

While Paul does not use the term "free will," he does make repeated statements about our ability to decide to accept or reject God's calling. For example, when he rebukes the Galatians for accepting a "gospel" other than the one true message of salvation, he writes that "I am astonished that you are so quickly deserting the one who called you to live in the grace of Christ and are turning to a different gospel" (Gal. 1:6). Again, in 2 Corinthians 11:3–4, Paul expresses concern that the believers in that church "may somehow be led astray from your sincere and pure devotion to Christ," because "if someone comes to you and preaches a Jesus other than the Jesus we preached, or if you receive a different spirit from the Spirit you received, or a different gospel from the one you accepted, you put up with it easily enough."

Paul seems to be saying that people whom God had called could decide to abandon their faith. More generally, Paul's instructions discussed throughout this book assume that his readers have the ability to decide whether to accept Christ and the gospel, whether to live in a holy manner that honors God, and whether to build healthy relationships as intended by God. In short, Paul's instructions indicate that we are free to make moral choices.

Yet, Paul also speaks forcefully about predestination. For example: "For he chose us in him before the creation of the world to be holy and blameless in his sight. In love he predestined us for adoption to sonship through Jesus Christ, in accordance with his pleasure and will" (Eph. 1:4–5). "In him we were also chosen, having been predestined according to the plan of him who works out everything in conformity with the purpose of his will" (Eph. 1:11). Further, Romans 9 is perhaps the most commonly cited chapter in Paul's letters for predestination. Paul addresses in that chapter why not all of the people of Israel have been saved. One of the reasons identified by Paul is God's sovereign choice:

> For he [God] says to Moses,
>   "I will have mercy on whom I have mercy, and I will have compassion on whom I have compassion."
>   It does not, therefore, depend on human desire or effort, but on God's mercy. (Rom. 9:15–16)

He continues in verse 18: "Therefore God has mercy on whom he wants to have mercy, and he hardens whom he wants to harden."

Significantly, while Romans 9 contains much that seems to support predestination, it ends with a discussion of what can be viewed as free will. In response to the question of why Israel had not attained righteousness although they pursued it (Rom. 9:30), Paul answers: "Why not? Because they pursued it not by faith but as if it were by works" (Rom. 9:32). In short, he points to their decision to pursue God through the law, rather than faith, as the reason why they failed to receive God's forgiveness and righteousness in Christ.

Paul simply doesn't seem to see an inconsistency between free will and predestination. While we may never understand fully how free will and predestination work harmoniously together, a possible starting point may be found in Paul's discussion of "objects of wrath." In Romans 9:22–24, Paul asks:

> What if God, although choosing to show his wrath and make his power known, bore with great patience the objects of his wrath—prepared for destruction? What if he did this to make the riches of his glory known to the objects of his mercy, whom he prepared in advance for glory—even us, whom he also called, not only from the Jews but also from the Gentiles?

While Paul does not answer directly whether some people were created to be objects of wrath, he does suggest strongly that God would have the right to do so if he so desired—and we would have no right to complain. This is certainly the point in Jeremiah 18 from which Paul seems to draw the inspiration for his discussion of "objects of wrath." In that passage, God instructs Jeremiah to go to a potter's house to observe a man forming a clay pot. "But the pot he was shaping from the clay was marred in his hands; so the potter formed it into another pot, shaping it as seemed best to him" (Jer. 18:4). Clearly stating the lesson from this event, Jeremiah reports in verses 5 and 6:

> Then the word of the LORD came to me. He said, "Can I not do with you, Israel, as this potter does?" declares the LORD. "Like

clay in the hand of the potter, so are you in my hand, Israel."

Although God declares clearly to Jeremiah that he has the power and right to reshape or even destroy us, God's declaration in the verses immediately following is equally clear regarding free will:

> If at any time I announce that a nation or kingdom is to be uprooted, torn down and destroyed, and if that nation I warned repents of its evil, then I will relent and not inflict on it the disaster I had planned. (Jer. 18:7–8)

The possibility that you can be transformed from an "object of wrath" into an "object of mercy" is also suggested in Paul's letter to the Ephesians. When writing to fellow believers whom he identified as being chosen by God before creation and predestined to be adopted as sons through Christ (Eph. 1:4–5), which clearly qualified them as "objects of mercy," Paul explains that they had been sinners along with the rest of humanity and: "Like the rest, we were by nature deserving of wrath" (Eph. 2:3). God had transformed these people who were "by nature deserving of wrath" (Eph. 2:3) into ones "predestined...for adoption to sonship through Jesus Christ" (Eph. 1:5).

The status of the Ephesian church is further addressed in Revelation 2:1–7 where Christ reprimands them for having "forsaken the love you had at first" and warns: "If you do not repent, I will come to you and remove your lampstand from its place" (Rev. 2:4–5). The church in Ephesus thus provides a case in point where the Scriptures seem to support both predestination and free will.

Although we may not understand how free will and predestination can coexist, our lack of comprehension does not change God's declaration of truth in his Word supporting both. The problem is not with God's Word, but with our limitations. Paul explains, as already discussed, that God stands above human understanding. God declares: "I will destroy the wisdom of the wise; the intelligence of the intelligent I will frustrate" (1 Cor. 1:19). Indeed, the very fact that we cannot understand fully all that God declares as true is to be expected because he is so much greater than us in every respect.

Consider a teacher or classmate in school who seemed to understand difficult concepts with ease while others struggled even to begin to grasp them. In the grand scheme of things, the difference between their intelligence and understanding was relatively small—perhaps a few IQ points or a few years of training—compared to the massive distance between human understanding and God. It is therefore hardly surprising that we cannot understand all of the harmonizing principles underlying what God declares and does. Perhaps in humility we need to accept God's declared truths rather than argue about what makes sense to us.

As a practical matter, we can draw at least two important life lessons from Paul's discussion of free will and predestination. One is that we should recognize God as sovereign who has the right to destroy or save as he sees fit. Stated differently, our attitude should be one of submission rather than entitlement. God calls to us in his grace and mercy but not because we are entitled to his grace and mercy.

A second practical lesson is that, in his mercy, God wants us to repent and accept the salvation he offers in Jesus Christ. We thus are morally responsible for how we respond to God's call. In short, rather than endlessly debating the various theories of free will and predestination, we should consider how Paul's instruction should practically affect our attitudes and actions here and now.

WHAT DO PAUL'S INSTRUCTIONS MEAN FOR US TODAY?

Pause and reflect on Paul's practical approach to points of theology. Use the following questions to consider carefully how his instructions should touch and transform your heart, mind, and life:

1. Why is it misguided to approach theology simply as a matter of intellectual curiosity about abstract principles? How does Paul's

practical approach to theology inform or challenge our approach to theology?

2. Do we tend to view theology as something best left to scholars? What is Paul's view on this point?

3. What points of theology are important to us? Why are they important to us?

4. How does our understanding of theology reflect or relate to the gospel? Are our theological views consistent with the gospel?

5. Are our theological convictions based on Scripture? Are they consistent with Scripture?

6. How does the gospel affect our understanding of baptism? What does it mean that we have been "baptized into Christ" and are "clothed...with Christ" (Gal. 3:27)?

7. When we take communion, do we remember and give thanks for Christ's sacrifice on the cross? How does this focus affect our attitude toward communion?

8. How can right beliefs guide right behavior?

9. How should our attitude and actions change in light of Paul's instruction on free will and predestination?

10. How should we think and live differently in light of Paul's practical approach to theology?

PART II: RIGHT CONDUCT

The gospel of Jesus Christ changes everything both for eternity and for our lives today. Here and now, the gospel should be transforming our lives. Thus, in this part of our study about right conduct, we begin in chapter 6 with Paul's call that we live up to the highest standard of holy living. We cannot achieve this holiness simply through our own efforts. Instead, as discussed in chapter 7, Christ and the Holy Spirit are at work in us to give us victory in the battle between our new and old natures. While there are many ways in which we can participate in putting our old sinful nature to death, Paul discusses at greatest length the importance of prayer (chapter 8), dealing properly with the ups and downs of life (chapter 9), and sexual purity (chapter 10). His practical instructions point the way to living the holy life to which we are called.

CHAPTER 6

Our High Calling to Holy Living

The two most significant events in all of human history—the death and resurrection of Jesus Christ—are at the heart of the gospel. On our own, we stand unworthy before God. Indeed, it is precisely because we are unworthy that Christ died for our sins. The Lord is perfect in holiness; we are wretched sinners.

Paul nevertheless calls us to the highest standard of holy living—a life worthy of the Lord and the gospel. Given that we are unworthy, how can Paul call us to live up to this standard of holiness? Rather than suggesting that we can do it on our own, Paul points to a deeper truth rooted in the gospel: Our risen Savior now lives in us and, through Christ, our lives can be transformed. Much as the work of Christ is the source of our salvation, his work within believers is the source of the power for the transformation of our lives.

WHAT IS THE STANDARD OF LIVING TO WHICH GOD IS CALLING US?

"Whatever happens, conduct yourself in a manner worthy of the gospel of Christ" (Phil. 1:27). "Live a life worthy of the Lord and please him in every way: bearing fruit in every good work, growing in the knowledge of God" (Col. 1:10). Paul prays that "our God may make you worthy of his calling" (2 Thess. 1:11). "Live a life worthy of the calling you have received" (Eph. 4:1). He also expresses confidence that "you will be counted worthy of the kingdom of God, for which you are suffering" (2 Thess. 1:5). He urges "you to live lives worthy of God, who calls you into his kingdom and glory" (1 Thess. 2:12).

These are more than lofty platitudes. As Paul makes clear, salvation must result in fundamental changes to our lives here and now. "So I tell you this, and insist on it in the Lord, that you must no longer live as the Gentiles do, in the futility of their thinking" (Eph. 4:17). God chose you "to be holy and blameless in his sight" (Eph. 1:4). You are "called to be his holy people" (1 Cor. 1:2). Paul's prayer is that "you will be blameless and holy in the presence of our God and Father when our Lord Jesus comes with all his holy ones" (1 Thess. 3:13). He urges us in Philippians 1:10 and 2:15 to be pure and blameless. Further, in light of God's promises, "let us purify ourselves from everything that contaminates body and spirit, perfecting holiness out of reverence for God" (2 Cor. 7:1). Paul's purpose is to "present everyone fully mature in Christ" (Col. 1:28).

While Paul states clearly that we can never earn salvation through good works, he is also clear that a proper and natural result of our faith in Christ is that our lives and lifestyles should change. Paul thus speaks of "your work produced by faith" (1 Thess. 1:3) and "every deed prompted by faith" (2 Thess. 1:11). "Everyone who confesses the name of the Lord must turn away from wickedness" (2 Tim. 2:19). In Ephesians 2:8–10, Paul explains:

> For it is by grace you have been saved, through faith—and this not from yourselves, it is the gift of God—not by works, so that no one can boast. *For we are God's handiwork, created in Christ Jesus to do good works, which God prepared in advance for us to do.*

In short, good works should be a natural—even necessary—result of our faith.

HOW CAN WE POSSIBLY LIVE A LIFE WORTHY OF GOD?

Paul does not simply set a high bar. The bar seems impossibly high: to be holy, blameless, worthy of the Lord and the gospel. It is inside this paradox that we encounter again the grace of God provided through Christ, without which the bar set by Paul would be absurd.

At the outset of this discussion, we need to see clearly that Paul never suggests we can live to this standard simply through personal effort and discipline. He in fact rebukes those who strive for holiness by submitting to a rigid set of rules ("Do not handle! Do not taste! Do not touch!"), which in Paul's words are "based on merely human commands and teaching" and which "have an appearance of wisdom, with their self-imposed worship, their false humility and their harsh treatment of the body, but they lack any value in restraining sensual indulgence" (Col. 2:21–23). In short, we will be doomed to frustration and failure if we seek to live holy lives through our own strength. This is not to say that holiness comes without effort (a topic discussed further in chapter 7 of our study). However, Paul points to a deeper truth that we need to understand as the foundation for personal holiness.

This deeper truth—what Paul describes as "the mystery that has been kept hidden for ages and generations, but is now disclosed to the Lord's people"—is *"Christ in you, the hope of glory"* (Col. 1:26–27). He repeats this point several times in different ways that reveal various dimensions of this fundamental truth. In Galatians 2:20, Paul declares: "I have been crucified with Christ and I no longer live, but Christ lives in me." We have "died with Christ to the elemental spiritual forces of this world" (Col. 2:20). Elaborating on the implications of being crucified with Christ, Paul explains in Romans 6:2–4 that:

> We are those who have died to sin; how can we live in it any longer? Or don't you know that all of us who were baptized into Christ Jesus were baptized into death? We were therefore buried with him through baptism into death in order that, just as Christ was raised from the dead through the glory of the Father, we too may live a new life.

Paul identifies "Christ in you" as the very test of the genuineness of our faith: "Examine yourselves to see whether you are in the faith; test yourselves. Do you not realize that Christ Jesus is in you—unless, of course, you fail the test? And I trust you will discover that we have not failed the test" (2 Cor. 13:5–6). Again, in Romans 8:9, Paul explains: "You, however, are not in the realm of the flesh but are in the realm of the Spirit, if indeed the Spirit of God lives in you. And if anyone does not have the Spirit of Christ, they do not belong to Christ."

Paul declares again and again that the Spirit of Christ dwells in every believer. In 1 Corinthians 3:16, he asks the pointed question: "Don't you know that you yourselves are God's temple and that God's Spirit dwells in your midst?" Again in 1 Corinthians 6:19–20:

> Do you not know that your bodies are temples of the Holy Spirit, who is in you, whom you have received from God? You are not your own; you were bought at a price. Therefore honor God with your bodies.

"For we are the temple of the living God" (2 Cor. 6:16). "God's temple is sacred, and you together are that temple" (1 Cor. 3:17).

The truth of "Christ in you" is both a present reality and a transforming process. The present reality is rooted firmly in the gospel message that once a person receives the gift of forgiveness and eternal life through faith in Christ, God no longer sees his or her sins but instead sees the righteousness of Christ who dwells in that individual. In addition to this present spiritual reality, there is an ongoing battle between our new nature in Christ and our old sinful nature (as discussed in the next chapter of our study). Through his eyes of mercy and grace, God sees Christ's righteousness in us now. But also our lives here and now should be in the process of being conformed to this eternal reality. This process cannot be accomplished through human effort, but only through "Christ in you, the hope of glory" (Col. 1:27).

Are we still Christians if we do not lead holy lives?

It is clear that a holy life worthy of God can be lived only through the power of "Christ in you" as we've just discussed. Our own efforts apart from Christ will never be sufficient. However, we reasonably ask what it means if we don't see a significant change in our lives and lifestyles after we declare Christ to be our Lord and Savior. Are we really Christians? Or are we immature Christians whose spiritual development has been stunted? Or are we works in progress who, with time, will experience the transforming work of Christ in our lives?

Because God alone can look into our hearts and know the sincerity of our faith, we can't expect Paul to answer these questions for an individual believer. However, he does provide key insights worthy of our careful consideration when reflecting on our individual situations.

In 1 Corinthians 3:11–15, Paul states plainly that a believer is saved so long as Christ is the foundation for his or her life even if that individual does not build properly on that foundation:

> For no one can lay any foundation other than the one already laid, which is Jesus Christ. If anyone builds on this foundation using gold, silver, costly stones, wood, hay or straw, their work will be shown for what it is, because the Day will bring it to light. It will be revealed with fire, and the fire will test the quality of each person's work. If what has been built survives, the builder will receive a reward. If it is burned up, the builder will suffer loss but yet will be saved—even though only as one escaping through the flames.

This truth flows naturally from the reality discussed in Part I of our study that our salvation is based on Christ, his death and resurrection—not our good works.

However, Paul is also clear that individuals who continue to practice sin are not part of God's kingdom. In 1 Corinthians 6:9–11, he explains:

Do you not know that *wrongdoers will not inherit the kingdom of God*? Do not be deceived: Neither the sexually immoral nor idolaters nor adulterers nor men who have sex with men nor thieves nor the greedy nor drunkards nor slanderers nor swindlers will inherit the kingdom of God. *And that is what some of you were. But you were washed, you were sanctified, you were justified in the name of the Lord Jesus Christ and by the Spirit of our God.*

Again, Galatians 5:19–21 declares:

The acts of the flesh are obvious: sexual immorality, impurity and debauchery; idolatry and witchcraft; hatred, discord, jealousy, fits of rage, selfish ambition, dissensions, factions and envy; drunkenness, orgies, and the like. I warn you, as I did before, that *those who live like this will not inherit the kingdom of God.*

Specifically addressing such conduct among those who call themselves Christians, Paul states in Ephesians 5:3–5 that:

But among you there must not be even a hint of sexual immorality, or of any kind of impurity, or of greed, because these are improper for God's holy people. Nor should there be obscenity, foolish talk or coarse joking, which are out of place, but rather thanksgiving. For of this you can be sure: *No immoral, impure or greedy person—such a person is an idolater—has any inheritance in the kingdom of Christ and of God.*

In the final analysis, God alone knows the reality of our faith, because he alone knows our hearts and deepest thoughts. While it can be difficult to be fully honest with ourselves, Paul instructs: "Examine yourselves to see whether you are in the faith; test yourselves" (2 Cor. 13:5). The test identified by Paul in this verse is whether "Christ Jesus is in you," and "you fail the test" if that is not the case (2 Cor. 13:5). The test is not how we compare to others or to subjective, self-centered standards. Regarding those who do so, Paul warns: "When they measure themselves by themselves and compare themselves with themselves, they are not wise" (2 Cor. 10:12).

Personal holiness reflects the reality of Christ in us. If we continue to practice sin as we did in the past, then we should consider carefully the genuineness of our faith. This point is made explicit in 1 John 3:6, 9:

> No one who lives in him [Christ] keeps on sinning. No one who continues to sin has either seen him or known him.... No one who is born of God will continue to sin, because God's seed remains in them; they cannot go on sinning, because they have been born of God.

This does not mean that Christians never sin. Indeed, this same book by John warns: "If we claim to be without sin, we deceive ourselves and the truth is not in us" (1 John 1:8). There is a difference between doing battle with sin (which is discussed in the next chapter of our study) and someone who "continues in sin" (1 John 3:6). In this instance, our claimed conversion has little or no effect on how we live today. Significantly, when discussing the problem of sin, John—like Paul—comes back to the gospel message of forgiveness in Christ. "If we confess our sins, he is faithful and just and will forgive us our sins and purify us from all unrighteousness" (1 John 1:9). As with so many questions that we confront in our daily walk, the answer to the problem of sin is Jesus Christ.

We are called to live holy lives worthy of the gospel, a task that is impossible when we try in our own wisdom and power. It becomes possible, even natural, through the work of Christ who dwells in every believer. When there is a gap between our calling and our present condition (and there always seems to be), we should consider prayerfully whether this gap reflects a reliance on ourselves rather than Christ, and even the deeper issue of the foundation on which our lives are built. A life built on the foundation of Christ is a life being transformed.

WHAT DO PAUL'S INSTRUCTIONS MEAN FOR US TODAY?

Pause and reflect on our high calling to holy living. Use the following questions to consider carefully how his instructions should touch and transform our hearts, minds, and lives:

1. How should the gospel change our lives and lifestyles? How has it affected our lives and lifestyles?

2. What does it mean to live a life "worthy of the gospel" (Phil. 1:27)?

3. How can we possibly live in a manner that is "holy and blameless in his [God's] sight" (Eph. 1:4)?

4. Why can't we achieve this standard for living by subjecting ourselves to rigid rules and discipline?

5. Why is it so tempting to fall back on our own effort again and again? How can we break that negative cycle?

6. How does the mystery of "Christ in you, the hope of glory" give us victory in our lives here and now? How does the presence of the Spirit of God in us empower us to live victoriously?

7. If we experience failure from time to time, should we simply give up? Why not?

8. Do we confess our sins and claim the forgiveness and victory that we can have in Christ?

9. Do we dwell in sin? Do we practice sin like a musician practices an instrument to get better and better? If so, what is our standing before God?

10. What specific changes need to be made to our lives and lifestyles in light of God's high calling to holy living?

CHAPTER 7

The Battle Between Our New and Old Natures

This is where the rubber meets the road. How can the spiritual reality of "Christ in you" become the personal experience of our lives today? A battle is waging in our hearts and minds between our new nature in Christ and our old sinful nature. In this chapter, we explore Paul's instructions on winning this battle. Ever persistent and a consummate tactician, Paul provides the strategies for victory in the power of Christ.

WHY DO WE STILL STRUGGLE WITH SIN IF CHRIST DWELLS IN US AND ALREADY HAS GIVEN US VICTORY?

As a starting point for answering this question, it is important to affirm again that Jesus Christ's crucifixion and resurrection—not our good works—are the basis for our salvation (chapter 1 of our study) and that Christ and the Spirit do in fact dwell in you (chapter 6). We are in fact new creations in Christ:

> Therefore, if anyone is in Christ, the new creation has come: The old has gone, the new is here! All this is from God, who reconciled us to himself through Christ and gave us the ministry of reconciliation: that God was reconciling the world to himself in Christ, not counting people's sins against them. And he has committed to us the message of reconciliation. (2 Cor. 5:17–19)

Yet, the reality that we are new creations in Christ does not mean that we suddenly escape the sin of our fallen world. Although God no longer counts our sin against us, we all can readily attest to our continuing struggle with sin. We thus can identify with Paul's description of his own struggle with sin:

> Although I want to do good, evil is right there with me. For in my inner being I delight in God's law; but I see another law at work in me, waging war against the law of my mind and making me a prisoner of the law of sin at work within me. What a wretched man I am! Who will rescue me from this body that is subject to death? Thanks be to God, who delivers me through Jesus Christ our Lord! So then, I myself in my mind am a slave to God's law, but in my sinful nature a slave to the law of sin. (Rom. 7:21–25)

Not only does Paul identify the source of our struggle in this passage—the battle between our new and old natures—but also the one and only possible source of victory in this battle: Jesus Christ our Lord.

When describing this transformation from our old sinful nature to the new nature we have in Christ, Paul uses the image of a person taking off a filthy set of clothes and putting on new clean clothes:

> You were taught, with regard to your former way of life, to put off your old self, which is being corrupted by its deceitful desires; to be made new in the attitude of your minds; and to put on the new self, created to be like God in true righteousness and holiness. (Eph. 4:22–24)

In Colossians 3:9–10, Paul again uses this imagery when he declares that "you have taken off your old self with its practices and have put on the new self, which is being renewed in knowledge in the image of its Creator." While these old clothes—our sinful nature—should be thrown away, we may be tempted to keep them in the closet and put them back on from time to time. We often do so out of habit. We might even try to wear both sets of clothes at the same time. This is at the core of the conflict between our old sinful nature and our new nature in Christ.

Paul discusses this ongoing conflict in considerable detail. In Galatians 5:17, Paul explains: "For the flesh desires what is contrary to the Spirit, and the Spirit what is contrary to the flesh. They are in conflict with each other, so that you are not to do whatever you want." Further emphasizing that our new and old natures are at war, Romans 8:5–8 instructs:

> Those who live according to the flesh have their minds set on what the flesh desires; but those who live in accordance with the Spirit have their minds set on what the Spirit desires. The mind governed by the flesh is death, but the mind governed by the Spirit is life and peace. The mind governed by the flesh is hostile to God; it does not submit to God's law, nor can it do so. Those who are in the realm of the flesh cannot please God.

This battle between our new and old natures is a reality for all believers. When we put our faith in Christ, he did not pull us instantaneously out of this world. We continue to struggle with sin both in the world and within ourselves. Rather than removing us from this battle, he gave us the Holy Spirit and made us a new creation in Christ—thus giving us the power and ultimate assurance of victory in this battle.

WHERE IS THE BATTLE FOUGHT?

The primary battleground is in our minds and hearts. While we might prefer to place the battle on the outside where it is not so personal, this war is being waged within our inner selves. "Those who live according to the flesh have their *minds* set on what the flesh *desires*" (Rom. 8:5). "The *mind* governed by the flesh is death, but the *mind* governed by the Spirit is life and peace. The *mind* governed by the flesh is hostile to God" (Rom. 8:6–7). "For the flesh *desires* what is contrary to the Spirit, and the Spirit what is contrary to the flesh" (Gal. 5:17). When discussing those who have rejected God, Paul refers to "the sinful *desires* of their hearts" (Rom. 1:24) and their "depraved *mind*" (Rom. 1:28).

Because the battle wages within our hearts and minds, we need to pay careful attention to what we desire and think. "Rather, clothe yourselves with the Lord Jesus Christ, and do not *think* about how to gratify the *desires* of the flesh" (Rom. 13:14). "So I say, walk by the Spirit, and you will not gratify the *desires* of the flesh" (Gal. 5:16). We are to stop "gratifying the *cravings* of our flesh and following its desires and *thoughts*" (Eph. 2:3). "Put to death, therefore, whatever belongs to your earthly nature: sexual immorality, impurity, *lust, evil desires and greed*, which is idolatry" (Col. 3:5). "Therefore do not let sin reign in your mortal body so that you obey its evil *desires*" (Rom. 6:12).

God wants to transform our minds so that we have the mind of Christ that does not dwell on sinful desires and thoughts. "Do not conform to the pattern of this world, but be transformed by the renewing of your *mind*" (Rom. 12:2). You are "to be made new in the attitude of your *minds*" (Eph. 4:23). "Have the same *mindset* as Christ Jesus" (Phil. 2:5). We are in fact "predestined to be conformed to the image of his Son" (Rom. 8:29) and even now we "are being transformed into his image" (2 Cor. 3:18). Indeed, "we have the *mind* of Christ" (1 Cor. 2:16).

We experience the mind of Christ as we think on things of God rather than things of this world. In Colossians 3:1–2, Paul calls us to "set your *hearts* on things above, where Christ is, seated at the right hand of God," and "set your *minds* on things above, not on earthly things." Again in Philippians 4:8, Paul instructs "whatever is true, whatever is noble, whatever is right, whatever is pure, whatever is lovely, whatever is admirable—if anything is excellent and praiseworthy—*think* about such things." "And the peace of God, which transcends all understanding, will guard your *hearts* and *minds* in Christ Jesus" (Phil 4:7).

All of Paul's talk about the transformation of our hearts and minds may make sense in theory, but what does it mean in practice? Do we have to give up what we think is fun for what we know is good? One of the mistaken assumptions underlying this type of question is that our old sinful nature does not know real joy. It focuses on immediate self-gratification without much concern about others or long-term consequences. As an extreme example, consider a drug addict who is always thinking about and yearning for her next hit. We all can see the folly of her ways and that if she could break the drug habit, her life would be better and happier. In a sense, the transformation of the believer's heart and mind is part of the process by which our addiction to sin is broken so that we can experience true life—now and throughout eternity—at a level far above what is possible with the old sinful nature.

WHAT IS THE SOURCE OF THE POWER
NEEDED TO WIN THIS BATTLE?

Because this battle is fought primarily within our hearts and minds, the source of the power needed for victory must also be internal. We typically think of weapons of war that we can see and touch—guns, tanks, planes and bombs. In contrast, we cannot physically see or touch the source of the power needed to win the battle between our old sinful nature and our new nature in Christ. And while human ingenuity or strategic planning can overcome a better equipped enemy in conventional warfare, our power source is not rooted in our personal ingenuity or cunning.

Instead, the Holy Spirit who dwells in us provides the power that we need to win this spiritual battle. In his letters to the churches, Paul refers repeatedly to the Spirit's power (Rom. 15:13, 19; 1 Cor. 2:4; Gal. 4:29; Eph. 3:16). We cannot win the battle between our new and old natures simply by relying on our own strength—after all, our human strength is part of our old nature that we have taken off! "For if you live according to the flesh, you will die; but if by the Spirit you put to death the misdeeds of the body, you will live. For those who are led by the Spirit of God are children of God" (Rom. 8:13–14). We "do not live according to the flesh but according to the Spirit" (Rom. 8:4). "Since we live by the Spirit, let us keep in step with the Spirit" (Gal. 5:25).

Paul repeatedly stresses the importance of the Spirit in the Christian walk. We are to be "filled with the Spirit" (Eph. 5:18), "and sanctified by the Holy Spirit" (Rom. 15:16). Indeed, in his letters to the churches, Paul refers to the Spirit nearly one hundred times. While we could have a separate chapter in this book on the Spirit, the reality is that Paul discusses the importance of the Spirit in every area of our Christian walk and, accordingly, the Spirit is an integral part of virtually every topic that we address.

Significantly, Paul does not describe the Spirit as an abstract force or vague concept. He instead uses personal terms full of emotion. We are "to please the Spirit" (Gal. 6:8). We are warned not to "grieve the Holy Spirit of God" (Eph. 4:30) and not to "quench the Spirit" (1 Thess. 5:19). While we can relate to God the Father and God the Son—since we're familiar with fathers and sons—the concept of God the Spirit may be more difficult to grasp. However, Paul describes the Spirit in very personal terms with emotions to which we can readily relate.

When describing the presence of God dwelling in believers, Paul seems to use interchangeably the terms "Christ in you" (Col. 1:27), "the Spirit of Christ" (Rom. 8:9), "God's Spirit" (1 Cor. 3:16) and "the Holy Spirit" (1 Cor. 6:19). While Paul does not use the word "Trinity," the unity of the Father, Son and Spirit is clear from Paul's letters. Indeed, the doctrine of the Trinity clearly reflects the "tri-unity" of the Father, Son, and Spirit identified by Paul.

And while there is a mystery to the Spirit, it is a mystery that should provide comfort as we recognize that God through the Spirit dwells in every believer and provides the power needed for victory in the battle between our old sinful nature and our new nature in Christ.

HOW DOES OUR SPEECH REFLECT THE STATUS OF THIS BATTLE?

The transformation of our minds and hearts should produce not only new patterns of conduct, but also new patterns of speech. As Christ declared: "For the mouth speaks what the heart is full of" (Matt. 12:34). "The things that come out of a person's mouth come from the heart"

(Matt. 15:18). Paul also identifies the close connection between what is in your heart and what comes out of your mouth:

> "The word is near you; it is in your *mouth* and in your *heart*," that is, the message concerning faith that we proclaim: If you declare with your *mouth*, "Jesus is Lord," and believe in your *heart* that God raised him from the dead, you will be saved. For it is with your *heart* that you believe and are justified, and it is with your *mouth* that you profess your faith and are saved. (Rom. 10:8–10)

In light of the close heart-mouth relationship, Paul stresses the need to monitor carefully what we say. "Do not let any unwholesome talk come out of your mouths, but only what is helpful for building others up according to their needs, that it may benefit those who listen" (Eph. 4:29). "Nor should there be obscenity, foolish talk or coarse joking, which are out of place, but rather thanksgiving" (Eph. 5:4). "It is shameful even to mention what the disobedient do in secret" (Eph. 5:12). "You must also rid yourselves of…slander, and filthy language from your lips" (Col. 3:8). "Get rid of…brawling and slander" (Eph. 4:31). "Do not lie to each other" (Col. 3:9). "Discord, jealousy, fits of rage, selfish ambition, slander, gossip, arrogance and disorder" (2 Cor. 12:20) should not be found among us.

Paul repeatedly lists slander among the sins deserving God's wrath (Rom. 1:30; 1 Cor. 5:11; 1 Cor. 6:10). When explaining the unrighteousness of all humanity, Paul quotes from the Psalms that "'their throats are open graves; their tongues practice deceit.' 'The poison of vipers is on their lips.' 'Their mouths are full of cursing and bitterness'" (Rom. 3:13–14). Clearly, Paul takes our words seriously—they aren't "just words," but external expressions of our internal condition.

Our words should bring life. We are called to bring "the message of reconciliation" to the world (2 Cor. 5:19). "Let your conversation be always full of grace, seasoned with salt, so that you may know how to answer everyone" (Col. 4:6). Within the church, Paul instructs that "with one mind and one voice" we are to "glorify the God and Father of our Lord Jesus Christ" (Rom. 15:6). He further instructs that we should be "speaking to one another with psalms, hymns, and songs from the Spirit" (Eph. 5:19). We are to "excel...in speech" (2 Cor. 8:7).

Our words can build up or tear down others. We can praise or dishonor God with our words. Not only does our speech have an external impact, but it also reflects the progress of Christ's work in us. As our hearts and minds are transformed by the work of Christ's Spirit within us, our patterns of speech will be lead indicators of that transformation. We should ever increasingly bless God and others in our speech.

IS THE OUTCOME OF THIS BATTLE IN DOUBT?

Spiritual and eternal victory is already assured. Once we have genuinely accepted the gospel in faith, we are "predestined to be conformed to the image of his Son" (Rom. 8:29). "For he chose us in him before the creation of the world to be holy and blameless in his sight" (Eph. 1:4). "He will also keep you firm to the end, so that you will be blameless on the day of our Lord Jesus Christ" (1 Cor. 1:8). We can have confidence in these promises because: "For no matter how many promises God has made, they are 'Yes' in Christ. And so through him the 'Amen' is spoken by us to the glory of God" (2 Cor. 1:20).

This victory is assured, not due to our strength but because of God's abundant resources. Paul's letter to the Ephesians makes this point again and again. God has "blessed us in the heavenly realms with every spiritual blessing in Christ" (Eph. 1:3). We have been redeemed "in accordance with the riches of God's grace that he lavished on us" (Eph. 1:7–8). We have hope in "the riches of his glorious inheritance in his holy people, and his incomparably great power for us who believe," and "that power is the same as the mighty strength he exerted when he raised Christ from the dead" (Eph. 1:18–20). "Because of his great love for us, God, who is rich in mercy, made us alive with Christ" (Eph. 2:4–5). He will show "the incomparable riches of his grace, expressed in his kindness to us in Christ

Jesus" (Eph. 2:7). "I pray that out of his glorious riches he may strengthen you with power through his Spirit in your inner being" (Eph. 3:16).

Paul prays further that you "grasp how wide and long and high and deep is the love of Christ, and to know this love that surpasses knowledge—that you may be filled to the measure of all the fullness of God" (Eph. 3:18–19). God is "able to do immeasurably more than all we ask or imagine, according to his power that is at work within us" (Eph. 3:20).

Given that our victory in Christ is assured, we might be tempted to kick back and disengage from the battle. But Paul gives the opposite instruction: Be fully engaged and fight the good fight. We therefore turn now to two famous illustrations provided by Paul describing how we participate in and experience victory in the battle between our new and old natures.

DOES THIS VICTORY RESULT FROM A NATURAL PROCESS OR DOES IT REQUIRE REAL EFFORT?

The two most famous images used by Paul when discussing Christian growth—"the fruit of the Spirit" (Gal. 5:22–23) and "the full armor of God" (Eph. 6:10–18)—reflect the reality that the victory of our new nature over our old nature involves both a natural internal process *and* external effort. On the one hand, fruit grows through a natural process beginning inside a properly rooted and nourished plant and then produces outward results. Similarly, the transformation of our minds and hearts should produce a natural outgrowth in new attitudes and actions. This reality is reflected in the organic image used by Paul in Galatians 5:22–23: "But the fruit of the Spirit is love, joy, peace, forbearance, kindness, goodness, faithfulness, gentleness and self-control." Similarly, in Ephesians 5:9, Paul declares that "the fruit of the light consists in all goodness, righteousness and truth."

On the other hand, a soldier must put on armor and does so to prepare for battle. This image emphasizes effort rather than an organic process of growth. It also focuses on external action rather than internal growth. Paul describes "the full armor of God" in Ephesians 6:10–17:

Finally, be strong in the Lord and in his mighty power. Put on the full armor of God, so that you can take your stand against the devil's schemes. For our struggle is not against flesh and blood, but against the rulers, against the authorities, against the powers of this dark world and against the spiritual forces of evil in the heavenly realms. Therefore put on the full armor of God, so that when the day of evil comes, you may be able to stand your ground, and after you have done everything, to stand. Stand firm then, with the belt of truth buckled around your waist, with the breastplate of righteousness in place, and with your feet fitted with the readiness that comes from the gospel of peace. In addition to all this, take up the shield of faith, with which you can extinguish all the flaming arrows of the evil one. Take the helmet of salvation and the sword of the Spirit, which is the word of God.

This armor metaphor is also used in 1 Thessalonians 5:8, which calls us to put on "faith and love as a breastplate, and the hope of salvation as a helmet." Paul again calls us to action with the exhortation to "continue to work out your salvation with fear and trembling, for it is God who works in you to will and to act in order to fulfill his good purpose" (Phil. 2:12–13). It is important to emphasize that neither the "work out your salvation" nor "full armor" passages, calls us to work in our own strength or with our own tools. It is God who works in us, and we are to wear the armor he has given us.

While the images of the "fruit of the Spirit" and the "full armor of God" may seem quite different, they together provide a balanced and practical guide on how to experience victory in our Christian walk. We are indeed called to holy lives that are worthy of the gospel and the power of the Spirit working in and through us to that effect. The battle between our old sinful nature and our new nature in Christ rages within our hearts and minds. Because of what God has done—and is doing—we have certain victory.

What do Paul's instructions mean for us today?

Pause and reflect on the battle between our old nature of sin and our new nature in Christ. Use the following questions to consider carefully Paul's instructions on the battle plan for victory:

1. Why do we sometimes seem to experience temporary defeat if Christ already has given us eternal victory?
2. What steps can we take to put our old nature to death?
3. What wrong patterns of behavior feed and thus strengthen our old nature? What do we need to do to change those self-destructive habits?
4. What steps can we take to experience the power of our new nature in Christ?
5. What food do we feed our minds? Does it strengthen our new nature or our old nature?
6. What programs do we watch on TV? What internet sites do we visit? What books, magazines and other materials do we read?
7. Are our daily priorities and practices focused on eternal goals or on immediate gratification? What changes do we need to make to our priorities and practices?
8. Do we see the fruit of the Spirit in our lives? If not, why not? If so, is the growth process increasing or decreasing?
9. Do we take the time and make the effort to put on the full armor of God? Are we ready for battle?
10. In light of the ongoing battle between our new and old natures, what do we need to do to live victoriously today?

Chapter 8

The Importance of Prayer

Prayer is a conversation with God. While some religions focus on rules and ritual, Christianity centers on the person of Jesus Christ. We cannot have a conversation with rules and rituals, but we can with a personal God. Just as communication is critical to a healthy relationship between any two individuals, prayer—communication with God—is critical to our relationship with Christ.

The importance of prayer flows logically from the foundational truths that we are saved through the person of Jesus Christ (as discussed in Part I of our study) and that we can live here and now as intended by God only through the work of the Spirit of Christ within us (as discussed in the earlier chapters of Part II). Because both our salvation and our spiritual growth are dependent on our personal relationship with God, communication through prayer is critical to that relationship. This distinctive quality of our faith provides the framework for Paul's instruction on prayer.

HOW OFTEN SHOULD WE PRAY?

We often pray at specific times—before meals, before bed, or when a particular need or praiseworthy event arises. But Paul is after something deeper when he speaks about prayer. Paul calls us to pray at all times and under all circumstances. We are to "pray continually, give thanks in all circumstances; for this is God's will for you in Christ Jesus" (1 Thess. 5:17–18). We are to be "faithful in prayer" (Rom. 12:12). "Devote yourselves to prayer, being watchful and thankful" (Col. 4:2). "Do not be anxious about anything, but in every situation, by prayer and petition, with thanksgiving, present your requests to God" (Phil. 4:6).

Not only does Paul instruct us to pray consistently and regularly, he also models this commitment to prayer. While we will review his prayers for the churches later in this chapter, here are some excerpts from Paul's description of his own prayer life:

- "God, whom I serve in my spirit in preaching the gospel of his Son, is my witness how *constantly I remember you in my prayers at all times*" (Rom. 1:9–10).
- "I *always* thank my God for you" (1 Cor. 1:4).
- "I have *not stopped* giving thanks for you, remembering you in my prayers" (Eph. 1:16).
- "I thank my God *every time* I remember you. In *all* my prayers for *all* of you, I *always* pray with joy" (Phil. 1:3–4).
- "We *always* thank God, the Father of our Lord Jesus Christ, when we pray for you" (Col. 1:3).
- "For this reason, since the day we heard about you, *we have not stopped praying for you*" (Col. 1:9).
- "We *always* thank God for all of you and *continually* mention you in our prayers. We remember before our God and Father your work produced by faith, your labor prompted by love, and your endurance inspired by hope in our Lord Jesus Christ" (1 Thess. 1:2–3).
- "And we also thank God *continually*" (1 Thess. 2:13).
- "We ought *always* to thank God for you, brothers and sisters, and rightly so" (2 Thess. 1:3).
- "With this in mind, we *constantly* pray for you" (2 Thess. 1:11).

Paul views prayer not only as an activity occurring at a point in time, but also as a state of being in which we dwell in God's presence through the Spirit. In the last chapter, we saw that living a holy life requires the power of the Spirit working within the believer. The same is true with maintaining a state of constant prayer. Through the Spirit, we can dwell continuously in God's presence—praying without ceasing.

WHAT IS THE ROLE OF THE SPIRIT IN OUR PRAYER LIVES?

Paul instructs us to pray with both our minds and our spirits. "So what shall I do? I will pray with my spirit, but I will also pray with my understanding; I will sing with my spirit, but I will also sing with my understanding" (1 Cor. 14:15). We partake of God as we pray in the Spirit. After explaining in Romans 8:23 that we "groan inwardly as we wait eagerly for our adoption to sonship, the redemption of our bodies," Paul continues in verses 26 and 27 to explain that:

> In the same way, the Spirit helps us in our weakness. We do not know what we ought to pray for, but the Spirit himself intercedes for us through wordless groans. And he who searches our hearts knows the mind of the Spirit, because the Spirit intercedes for God's people in accordance with the will of God.

In Ephesians 6:18, he further instructs: "And pray in the Spirit on all occasions with all kinds of prayers and requests. With this in mind, be alert and always keep on praying for all the Lord's people." We have "access to the Father by one Spirit" (Eph. 2:18). We "worship by the Spirit of God" (Phil. 3:3, NIV 1984). Paul is clear that the Spirit is central to our prayer lives.

The Spirit also provides for an intimacy in prayer. Paul explains that "the Spirit you received brought about your adoption to sonship. And by him we cry, 'Abba, Father.' The Spirit himself testifies with our spirit that we are God's children" (Rom. 8:15–16). "Abba" is an Aramaic word that might be best translated into English as "Daddy," which reflects the intimate relationship that a child has with his or her father. Paul uses this same word in Galatians 4:6, where he declares: "Because you are his sons, God sent the Spirit of his Son into our hearts, the Spirit who calls out, 'Abba, Father.'" We experience intimacy with God through the Spirit in our prayer lives.

WHAT ABOUT PRAYING IN "TONGUES"?

The spiritual gift of tongues is one expression of praying in the spirit. Paul explains: "For if I pray in a tongue, my spirit prays, but my mind is unfruitful" (1 Cor. 14:14). "For anyone who speaks in a tongue does not speak to people but to God. Indeed, no one understands them; they utter mysteries by the Spirit" (1 Cor. 14:2). In 1 Corinthians 12–14 (which contains the only discussion of tongues in Paul's letters), Paul seems to identify three different expressions of the gift of tongues: (1) prayer tongues in which our spirits are engaged with the Spirit (discussed in the text above); (2) tongues as a sign to unbelievers (1 Cor. 14:22, and perhaps seen best in operation at Pentecost as reported in Acts 2); and (3) tongues that, with an interpretation, edify the church (1 Cor. 14:5–6).

Despite the rhetoric that we may hear on one side or the other of this sometimes contentious subject, Paul makes both positive and negative statements about tongues. In 1 Corinthians 14:18, he declares: "I thank God that I speak in tongues more than all of you." And while he indicates that tongues are but one of many spiritual gifts and not all Christians have the gift of tongues (1 Cor. 12:7–11, 28–31), Paul also states: "I would like every one of you to speak in tongues, but I would rather have you prophesy" (1 Cor. 14:5).

He also warns about the misuse and excessive emphasis on tongues. Paul views other spiritual gifts as more important than tongues (1 Cor. 14:1–5) and warns against the improper and disorderly use of tongues (1 Cor. 14:6–25). While recognizing the potential for misuse, he concludes by directing specifically: "Do not forbid speaking in tongues. But everything should be done in a fitting and orderly way" (1 Cor. 14:39–40).

We, too, should have a balanced perspective on tongues. It is misguided to either overemphasize or ignore this subject. Perhaps most importantly, we should not treat this subject as simply an abstract matter to be debated. It has practical relevance to our prayer lives, which in turn is important to our relationship with God through Jesus Christ. The proper balance is suggested by Paul when he calls us to pray with our minds and our spirits (1 Cor. 14:15).

WHAT ARE PAUL'S INSTRUCTIONS ABOUT PRAISING GOD?

Praise should be a major part of our prayers. "Rejoice in the Lord always. I will say it again: Rejoice!" (Phil. 4:4). Not only does Paul call us to praise God, he also models that behavior. He often bursts out in praise to God in his letters. At times, he pauses briefly to praise God in the middle of a sentence on another topic. For example, when discussing humanity's rejection of God in Romans 1:25, Paul writes: "They exchanged the truth about God for a lie, and worshiped and served created things rather than *the Creator—who is forever praised. Amen.*" Again, in Romans 9:5 when discussing God's blessings on the people of Israel, he states that "from them is traced the human ancestry of *the Messiah, who is God over all, forever praised! Amen.*" He declares in 2 Corinthians 11:31 that: "*The God and Father of the Lord Jesus, who is to be praised forever*, knows that I am not lying." We can learn from Paul's example of pausing to praise God whenever the opportunity permits.

In addition to these mid-sentence outbursts of praise, Paul laces his letters with other declarations of praise to God:

- "For from him and through him and for him are all things. To him be the glory forever! Amen" (Rom. 11:36).
- "Now to him who is able to establish you in accordance with my gospel, the message I proclaim about Jesus Christ, in keeping with the revelation of the mystery hidden for long ages past, but now revealed and made known through the prophetic writings by the command of the eternal God, so that all the Gentiles might come to the obedience that comes from faith—to the only wise God be glory forever through Jesus Christ! Amen!" (Rom. 16:25–27).
- "Praise be to the God and Father of our Lord Jesus Christ, the

Father of compassion and the God of all comfort" (2 Cor. 1:3).

- "Praise be to the God and Father of our Lord Jesus Christ, who has blessed us in the heavenly realms with every spiritual blessing in Christ" (Eph. 1:3).

- When observing that some preach the gospel with questionable motives, Paul notes that "Christ is preached" and "because of this I rejoice. Yes, and I will continue to rejoice" (Phil. 1:18).

We bring praise to God not only with our words, but also through our actions. Paul explains in Romans 15:7 that: "Accept one another, then, just as Christ accepted you, in order to bring praise to God." Again he writes: "Because of the service by which you have proved yourselves, others will praise God for the obedience that accompanies your confession of the gospel of Christ, and for your generosity in sharing with them and with everyone else" (2 Cor. 9:13). In Philippians 1:9–11, Paul prays that the believers might grow in love, knowledge, insight, discernment, purity and righteousness "to the glory and praise of God." Indeed, suggesting that our very being as Christians brings praise and glory to God, Paul declares that our adoption as God's children through Jesus Christ is "to the praise of his glorious grace," God's decision to choose us is "for the praise of his glory," and God's grant of his Spirit to us is "to the praise of his glory" (Eph. 1:6, 12, 14).

In word and deed, our lives should overflow with praise to God. Praise should season our conversations with others. When we pray, our praise springs from the Spirit to build our relationship with God through Christ. And in our daily lives, our actions and very being serve as living praise to God. Life in Christ is a life of praise. In Paul's words: "Rejoice in the Lord always. I will say it again: Rejoice!" (Phil. 4:4).

HOW DID PAUL PRAY FOR OTHER BELIEVERS?

In addition to praising God for who he is and what he has done, Paul prayed diligently for the churches. As we survey Paul's prayers in the next few pages, we begin by reviewing his prayers of thanksgiving for God's work in their lives. We then will turn to his prayers of petition for their continued spiritual growth, and finally to his prayers for God's blessings on their lives. Due to the large volume of verses reflecting Paul's prayers for believers, we will make generous use of lists that can be read to help appreciate Paul's heart of prayer for others. We should reflect on our own prayer lives as we consider Paul's example of how he prayed for other believers.

Prayers of Thanksgiving. Paul's heart overflowed with thanks for God's work among the believers. Although these believers were far from perfect (as apparent from the many corrections and admonitions from Paul provided in his letters to them), Paul nevertheless recognized that God was at work in their lives and gave thanks to God as reflected in the following passages:

- "First, I thank my God through Jesus Christ for all of you, because your faith is being reported all over the world" (Rom. 1:8).
- "I always thank my God for you because of his grace given you in Christ Jesus. For in him you have been enriched in every way—with all kinds of speech and with all knowledge—God thus confirming our testimony about Christ among you" (1 Cor. 1:4–6).
- "For this reason, ever since I heard about your faith in the Lord Jesus and your love for all God's people, I have not stopped giving thanks for you, remembering you in my prayers" (Eph. 1:15–16).
- "I thank God every time I remember you" (Phil. 1:3).
- "We always thank God, the Father of our Lord Jesus Christ,

when we pray for you, because we have heard of your faith in Christ Jesus and of the love you have for all God's people—the faith and love that spring from the hope stored up for you in heaven and about which you have already heard in the true message of the gospel that has come to you" (Col. 1:3–6).

- "We always thank God for all of you and continually mention you in our prayers. We remember before our God and Father your work produced by faith, your labor prompted by love, and your endurance inspired by hope in our Lord Jesus Christ" (1 Thess. 1:2–3).

- "And we also thank God continually because, when you received the word of God, which you heard from us, you accepted it not as a human word, but as it actually is, the word of God" (1 Thess. 2:13).

- "How can we thank God enough for you in return for all the joy we have in the presence of our God because of you?" (1 Thess. 3:9).

- "We ought always to thank God for you, brothers and sisters, and rightly so, because your faith is growing more and more, and the love all of you has for one another is increasing" (2 Thess. 1:3).

- "But we ought always to thank God for you, brothers and sisters loved by the Lord, because God chose you as firstfruits to be saved through the sanctifying work of the Spirit and through belief in the truth" (2 Thess. 2:13).

We should be challenged in our prayer lives by Paul's heart of thanksgiving when praying for other believers. Unlike Paul, our prayers tend to focus on ourselves rather than others. And when we pray about others, we're more likely to ask God to change them rather than thank God for how he is working in them. Our attitudes and relationships would be very different—and much better—if we spent more time thanking God for his work in the lives of others.

Prayers for Spiritual Growth. While thankful for what God already had done in the lives of believers, Paul also prayed fervently for their continued growth in the faith. His prayers for spiritual growth were specific and passionate. We should consider, once again, how the following prayers of Paul provide an example for our prayer lives:

- "Now we pray to God that you will not do anything wrong… and our prayer is that you may be fully restored" (2 Cor. 13:7–9).

- "I keep asking that the God of our Lord Jesus Christ, the glorious Father, may give you the Spirit of wisdom and revelation, so that you may know him better. I pray that the eyes of your heart may be enlightened in order that you may know the hope to which he has called you, the riches of his glorious inheritance in his holy people, and his incomparably great power for us who believe" (Eph. 1:17–19).

- "For this reason I kneel before the Father, from whom every family in heaven and on earth derives its name. I pray that out of his glorious riches he may strengthen you with power through his Spirit in your inner being, so that Christ may dwell in your hearts through faith. And I pray that you, being rooted and established in love, may have power, together with all the Lord's holy people, to grasp how wide and long and high and deep is the love of Christ, and to know this love that surpasses knowledge—that you may be filled to the measure of all the fullness of God" (Eph. 3:14–19).

- "In all my prayers for all of you, I always pray with joy because of your partnership in the gospel from the first day until now, being confident of this, that he who began a good work in you will carry it on to completion until the day of Christ Jesus" (Phil. 1:4–6).

- "And this is my prayer: that your love may abound more and more in knowledge and depth of insight, so that you may be able to discern what is best and may be pure and blameless for the day of Christ, filled with the fruit of righteousness that comes through Jesus Christ—to the glory and praise of God" (Phil. 1:9–11).

- "For this reason, since the day we heard about you, we have not stopped praying for you. We continually ask God to fill you with the knowledge of his will through all the wisdom and understanding that the Spirit gives, so that you may live a life worthy of the Lord and please him in every way: bearing fruit in every good work, growing in the knowledge of God, being strengthened with all power according to his glorious might so that you may have great endurance and patience, and giving joyful thanks to the Father, who has qualified you to share in the inheritance of his holy people in the kingdom of light" (Col. 1:9–12).

- "Night and day we pray most earnestly that we may see you again and supply what is lacking in your faith" (1 Thess. 3:10).

- "May the Lord make your love increase and overflow for each other and for everyone else, just as ours does for you. May he strengthen your hearts so that you will be blameless and holy in the presence of our God and Father when our Lord Jesus comes with all his holy ones" (1 Thess. 3:12–13).

- "May God himself, the God of peace, sanctify you through and through. May your whole spirit, soul and body be kept blameless at the coming of our Lord Jesus Christ" (1 Thess. 5:23).

- "With this in mind, we constantly pray for you, that our God may make you worthy of his calling, and that by his power he may bring to fruition your every desire for goodness and your every deed prompted by faith. We pray this so that the name of our Lord Jesus may be glorified in you, and you in him, according to the grace of our God and the Lord Jesus Christ" (2 Thess. 1:11–12).

- "May our Lord Jesus Christ himself and God our Father, who loved us and by his grace gave us eternal encouragement and good hope, encourage your hearts and strengthen you in every good deed and word" (2 Thess. 2:16–17).

From his prayers, we can sense the intensity of Paul's passion for the spiritual growth of all believers. His desire is not merely that we stay out of trouble. He prays that we will be "filled to the measure of all the fullness of God" (Eph. 3:19), that we attain to "the whole measure of the fullness of Christ" (Eph. 4:13), that our love "may abound more and more in knowledge and depth of insight" (Phil. 1:9), that we be filled with "the knowledge of his will through all the wisdom and understanding that the Spirit gives" (Col. 1:9), that we be "blameless and holy in the presence of our God and Father" (1 Thess. 3:13), and that we be strengthened "in every good deed and word" (2 Thess. 2:17).

Do we display this passion in our prayers for others? Do we even pray for others except when they are sick or in dire circumstances? While we certainly should pray for those in need, Paul provides an example of praying for spiritual victory, not just survival. And he also prayed that he could be there to help them on their spiritual journey. "God, whom I serve in my spirit in preaching the gospel of his Son, is my witness how consistently I remember you in my prayers at all times; and I pray now at last by God's will the way may be opened for me to come to you" (Rom. 1:9–10). "Now may our God and Father himself and our Lord Jesus clear the way for us to come to you" (1 Thess. 3:11). We too should pray passionately for spiritual growth of other believers and that we may be used by God to aid in that growth.

Prayers of Blessing. Among Paul's first words in each of his letters to the churches is a blessing of God's grace and peace:

- "Grace and peace to you from God our Father and from the Lord Jesus Christ" (Rom. 1:7).
- "Grace and peace to you from God our Father and the Lord Jesus Christ" (1 Cor. 1:3).
- "Grace and peace to you from God our Father and the Lord Jesus Christ" (2 Cor. 1:2).
- "Grace and peace to you from God our Father and the Lord Jesus Christ, who gave himself for our sins to rescue us from the present evil age, according to the will of our God and Father, to

whom be glory for ever and ever. Amen" (Gal. 1:3–5).

- "Grace and peace to you from God our Father and the Lord Jesus Christ" (Eph. 1:2).
- "Grace and peace to you from God our Father and the Lord Jesus Christ" (Phil. 1:2).
- "Grace and peace to you from God our Father" (Col. 1:2).
- "Grace and peace to you" (1 Thess. 1:1).
- "Grace and peace to you from God the Father and the Lord Jesus Christ" (2 Thess. 1:2).

He also sprinkles blessings elsewhere in his letters. "May the grace of the Lord Jesus Christ, and the love of God, and the fellowship of the Holy Spirit be with you all" (2 Cor. 13:14). "The grace of our Lord Jesus Christ be with your spirit, brothers and sisters. Amen" (Gal. 6:18). "Now may the Lord of peace himself give you peace at all times and in every way. The Lord be with all of you" (2 Thess. 3:16). "The grace of our Lord Jesus Christ be with you all" (2 Thess. 3:18).

This practice of blessing others seems lost today. Even with close friends, we're more likely to give a casual or even sarcastic greeting. Paul's example should encourage us to speak words of blessing that may be as simple as a word of encouragement. Or, as the opportunity presents itself, we can affirm others in their walk in Christ or tell them that we are praying for them. In short, we should be a blessing to others.

DOES PRAYER CHANGE ANYTHING?

Paul states clearly that prayer makes a positive difference. In Romans 15:30, he pleads: "I urge you, brothers and sisters, by our Lord Jesus Christ and by the love of the Spirit, to join me in my struggle by praying to God for me." In 2 Corinthians 1:10–11, Paul declares with confidence that God "has delivered us from such a deadly peril," and that "he will continue to deliver us, as you help us by your prayers." In Ephesians 6:19–20, he requests:

Pray also for me, that whenever I speak, words may be given me so that I will fearlessly make known the mystery of the gospel, for which I am an ambassador in chains. Pray that I may declare it fearlessly, as I should.

Again, in 2 Thessalonians 3:1–2, Paul states:

Pray for us that the message of the Lord may spread rapidly and be honored, just as it was with you. And pray that we may be delivered from wicked and evil people, for not everyone has faith.

We don't pray simply to make ourselves feel better. When we pray, we are talking with the living God who is all powerful and full of love for us. Through the Spirit, we engage God at a deep level where we bring our praise and petitions. Paul's own example of prayer demonstrates that he was persuaded that his prayers had a concrete impact for good. We, too, can come before God with confidence that our prayers make a real difference.

WHAT DO PAUL'S INSTRUCTIONS MEAN FOR US TODAY?

Pause and reflect on the importance of prayer. Use the following questions to consider carefully Paul's instruction and example on this subject:

1. How often do we pray? Do we need to set aside more time for prayer?
2. What would it mean to be in a constant state of prayer? What fills our minds when we are not focusing on anything in particular? Does God fill those gaps?
3. Do we pray with both our minds and spirits? Do we use a list of issues and concerns during our prayers? Do we also take time

simply to sit in God's presence and be led by the Spirit?

4. What role, if any, does the spiritual gift of tongues have in our prayer lives?

5. Do we spend time praising God for who he is and what he has done? During the course of the day, are there moments when we feel like bursting out with praise? Do we do it?

6. Do we use notes or other prompts to remind us to pray (like a sticky note on our computer screens)? What reminders to pray might we use?

7. Do we have prayer partners or a small group of fellow believers with whom we pray? Would praying more with others encourage our personal prayer lives?

8. Does prayer make a difference? How would our prayer lives be different if we really believed that our prayers made a difference?

9. Do we pray regularly and passionately for missionaries and other Christian workers who are spreading the gospel?

10. How should the importance of prayer affect how we think and what we do?

CHAPTER 9

The Ups and Downs of Life

Nowhere does Paul suggest that Christians are immune from health problems, family difficulties, financial setbacks, or the other ups and downs of life. Sometimes, the downs can feel so low that they test our faith and character. Human-defined highs can also be dangerous—often even more than the lows of life—because we may come to rely on ourselves or material resources rather than God.

Paul experienced more ups and downs than we are likely to ever experience, so he knew firsthand how to be content during life's difficulties and learn from them. He also understood that human accomplishments, no matter how great, pale in comparison to the surpassing work of Christ in our lives. We can learn from both his instructions and example.

HOW CAN WE STAND FIRM AND BE CONTENT UNDER ALL CIRCUMSTANCES?

Based on his firsthand experience, Paul declares in Philippians 4:11–13 the secret to contentment throughout life's ups and downs:

> I have learned to be content whatever the circumstances. I know what it is to be in need, and I know what it is to have plenty. I have learned the secret of being content in any and every situation, whether well fed or hungry, whether living in plenty or in want. *I can do all this through him who gives me strength.*

Paul understood that this is an ongoing reality, regardless of the shape of his circumstances. "And the peace of God, which transcends all understanding, will guard your hearts and mind in Christ Jesus" (Phil. 4:7).

This secret of contentment differs markedly from the self-help programs we see marketed on infomercials. Godly contentment does not involve a get-rich-quick scheme or learning self-reliance. Material possessions, good looks, good health or good feelings cannot keep us content for long because they all fade and fail. The search for worldly contentment is a never-ending and exhausting chase. Paul thus directs us to the one who will never fade or fail. The secret of true contentment is Jesus Christ. It is Christ who saves us (chapter 1 of our study) and Christ who resides in us and empowers us to live the life to which we are called (chapter 6). For the Christian, Christ himself is the ultimate answer to the basic questions of life.

Thus, in his letters, Paul repeatedly calls us to "stand firm" in Christ no matter the circumstances:

- "Therefore, my dear brothers and sisters, *stand firm*. Let nothing move you" (1 Cor. 15:58).
- "Be on your guard; *stand firm* in the faith; be courageous; be strong" (1 Cor. 16:13).
- "Now it is God who makes both us and you *stand firm* in Christ" (2 Cor. 1:21).
- "It is by faith you *stand firm*" (2 Cor. 1:24).
- "*Stand firm*, then, and do not let yourselves be burdened again by a yoke of slavery" (Gal. 5:1).
- "*Stand firm* then, with the belt of truth buckled around your waist" as well as the rest of the full armor of God (Eph. 6:14).
- "I will know that you will *stand firm* in the one Spirit" (Phil. 1:27).
- "That you may *stand firm* in all the will of God, mature and fully assured" (Col. 4:12).
- "For now we really live, since you are *standing firm* in the Lord" (1 Thess. 3:8).
- "So then, brothers and sisters, *stand firm* and hold fast to the

teachings we passed on to you, whether by word of mouth or by letter." (2 Thess. 2:15)

Christ does not promise that our lives will always be easy. He does promise, however, to always be with us and in us. That is the foundation on which we can stand firm and be content no matter the circumstances. When we are content in Christ, the storms of life cannot shake our firm foundation. We may be sad, of course, if we lose a loved one or a job, or if we suffer some other setback. However, because our lives are not built on our job or other "thing," these losses do not alter the surpassing reality that we remain secure in Christ—now and through all eternity.

HOW SHOULD WE VIEW OUR HUMAN ACCOMPLISHMENTS?

We often place great value on our accomplishments. Since we worked hard for them, we may become proud and boastful. Yet, compared to the all-surpassing worth of Christ's work on the cross and in our lives, our human accomplishments have little value and provide no basis for boasting. Using the standards of success in the Jewish culture of his day, Paul had reason to take pride in himself. In Philippians 3:4–6, Paul explains:

> If someone else thinks they have reasons to put confidence in the flesh, I have more: circumcised on the eighth day, of the people of Israel, of the tribe of Benjamin, a Hebrew of Hebrews; in regard to the law, a Pharisee; as for zeal, persecuting the church; as for righteousness based on the law, faultless.

He had received training from one of the most respected Jewish rabbis of the first century (Acts 22:3) and "conformed to the strictest sect of our [Jewish] religion" (Acts 26:5). Yet, despite everything about which he could have boasted, Paul "consider[ed] them garbage" and "a loss because of the surpassing worth of knowing Christ Jesus my Lord" (Phil. 3:8).

Consistent with Paul's example, we should not boast about our accomplishments. "Your boasting is not good" (1 Cor. 5:6). Paul includes those who are "arrogant and boastful" along with "God-haters" and others with a "depraved mind" (Rom. 1:28–31). Moreover, when listing the qualities of love, he states that love "does not boast" (1 Cor. 13:4). As we stand before God, we have no cause to boast because our salvation is not based on works but on faith in Christ. Such boasting is "excluded" (Rom. 3:27), "no one may boast before him" (1 Cor. 1:29), and "no one can boast" (Eph. 2:9). Rather than boasting about his accomplishments, Paul declares: "If I must boast, I will boast of the things that show my weakness" (2 Cor. 11:30). "Therefore I will boast all the more gladly about my weaknesses, so that Christ's power may rest on me" (2 Cor. 12:9).

Our pride in human accomplishments—what Paul calls "confidence in the flesh" (Phil. 3:4)—is a barrier to our growth in Christ. God did not choose us based on our accomplishments or credentials. Indeed:

God chose the foolish things of the world to shame the wise;
God chose the weak things of the world to shame the strong.
God chose the lowly things of this world and the despised
things—and the things that are not—to nullify things that are,
so that no one may boast before him. (1 Cor. 1:27–29)

We did not earn God's favor, but received it as a gift. "And if you did receive it, why do you boast as though you did not?" (1 Cor. 4:7).

Thus, if we boast, we should boast in the Lord. "May I never boast except in the cross of our Lord Jesus Christ, through which the world has been crucified to me, and I to the world" (Gal. 6:14). "Therefore, as it is written: 'Let the one who boasts boast in the Lord'" (1 Cor. 1:31). He repeats in 2 Corinthians 10:17 that: "Let the one who boasts boast in the Lord." He also boasts of what God is doing in his life (2 Cor. 1:12), and even more about what God is doing in the lives of other Christians. As Paul reports in 2 Thessalonians 1:4: "Among God's churches we boast about your perseverance and faith in all persecutions and trials you are enduring." Other passages in which Paul seeks to build up others by boasting about God's work in their lives include 2 Corinthians 1:14; 2 Corinthians 7:14; and 2 Corinthians 9:2–3.

In short, Paul turns the world's approach to pride and boasting on its head. Rather than boasting about who we are or what we have accomplished, we are to boast of who God is and what he is doing in the lives of others.

WHAT IS THE ROLE OF SUFFERING IN A CHRISTIAN'S LIFE?

Paul's view of suffering is also at odds with the commonly held view today that it should be avoided at all costs. He in fact provides a long list of examples of how suffering for the sake of Christ produces good:

- "We also glory in our sufferings, because we know that *suffering produces perseverance*; perseverance, character; and character, hope" (Rom. 5:3–4).

- "Now if we are children, then we are heirs—heirs of God and co-heirs with Christ, if indeed we *share in his sufferings* in order that we may also share in his glory. I consider that our present sufferings are not worth comparing with the glory that will be revealed in us" (Rom. 8:17–18).

- "We are hard pressed on every side, but not crushed; perplexed, but not in despair; persecuted, but not abandoned; struck down, but not destroyed. We always carry around in our body the death of Jesus, *so that the life of Jesus may also be revealed in our body.* For we who are alive are always being given over to death for Jesus' sake, *so that his life may also be revealed in our mortal body*" (2 Cor. 4:8–11).

- Paul praises "the Father of compassion and the God of all comfort, who *comforts us in all our troubles, so that we can comfort those in any trouble with the comfort we ourselves have receive from God.*

For just as we share abundantly in the sufferings of Christ, so also our comfort abounds through Christ. If we are distressed, it is for your comfort and salvation; if we are comforted, it is for your comfort, which produces in you *patient endurance of the same sufferings we suffer*. And our hope for you is firm, because we know that just as you share in our sufferings, so also you share in our comfort" (2 Cor. 1:3–7).

- "For our light and momentary troubles are achieving for us an *eternal glory* that far outweighs them all" (2 Cor. 4:17).

- "Now I want you to know, brothers and sisters, that what has happened to me has really served to *advance the gospel*.... And because of my chains, most of the brothers and sisters have *become more confident* in the Lord and dare all the more to *proclaim the gospel without fear*" (Phil. 1:12, 14).

- "For it has been granted to you to on behalf of Christ not only to believe in him, but also to *suffer for him*" (Phil. 1:29).

- "I want to know Christ—yes, to know the power of his resurrection and *participation in his sufferings*, becoming like him in his death, and so, somehow, attaining to the resurrection from the dead" (Phil. 3:10–11).

- "All this is evidence that God's judgment is right, and as a result you will be counted as *worthy of the kingdom of God, for which you are suffering*" (2 Thess. 1:5).

In summary, Paul urges us to rejoice in suffering for Christ's sake because it brings many benefits including: (1) developing Christian character including perseverance; (2) providing evidence that we are co-heirs with Christ and will share in his glory; (3) revealing Christ's power in our weak bodies; (4) allowing us to experience God's comfort, which enables us to comfort others; (5) achieving for us an eternal glory; (6) advancing the spread of the gospel; and (7) experiencing the privilege of suffering for Christ and his kingdom.

Paul does not say that suffering will be easy. However, when God allows suffering in our lives, he will be with us and bring about good—

not just despite our suffering but actually through it. Our perspective should stand in stark contrast to the world's avoid-at-all-costs approach to suffering.

SHOULD WE SEEK TO SUFFER?

Nowhere does Paul state that we should seek to suffer or inflict pain on our bodies based on a misguided belief that it might facilitate spiritual growth. To the contrary, he condemns those who would engage in the "harsh treatment of the body"—including this type of conduct along with "self-imposed worship" and "false humility"—as practices that may have "an appearance of wisdom…but they lack any value in restraining sensual indulgence" (Col. 2:23). These are "rules, which have to do with things that are all destined to perish with use, are based on human commands and teachings" (Col. 2:22).

There is a place, of course, for learning self-denial. As discussed in chapter 7, Paul instructs us not to feed the appetites of our sinful natures. He also calls us to be like an athlete who engages in strict training of the body (1 Cor. 9:25–27). However, proper self-discipline is a far cry from intentionally injuring our bodies. We certainly can learn from the suffering that God, in his sovereignty, allows into our lives, without inflicting unnecessary suffering on ourselves.

WHAT WAS PAUL'S EXPERIENCE WITH SUFFEERING?

Paul speaks about suffering from his firsthand experience. In 2 Corinthians 11:24–27, he recounts:

> Five times I received from the Jews the forty lashes minus one. Three times I was beaten with rods, once I was pelted with stones, three times I was shipwrecked, I spent a night and a day in the open sea, I have been constantly on the move. I have been

in danger from rivers, in danger from bandits, in danger from my fellow Jews, in danger from Gentiles; in danger in the city, in danger in the country, in danger at sea; and in danger from false believers. I have labored and toiled and have often gone without sleep; I have known hunger and thirst and have often gone without food; I have been cold and naked.

In this passage, he is not complaining about suffering, but is rather explaining to the Corinthian believers that, as they consider the credibility of his message, they should see his willingness to suffer for the sake of spreading the gospel as evidence of the faithfulness of his service and the integrity of his teaching. This is also reflected in 2 Corinthians 6:3–10; 2 Corinthians 7:2–7; 2 Corinthians 11:16 to 12:10. In these passages, Paul engages in ironic boasting about his ministry and suffering—not out of pride, but out of a desire for the Corinthians to realize that the message brought by Paul is more reliable than false teachers who were concerned primarily about their own interests.

In perhaps his most personal discussion of suffering, Paul describes his experience with "a thorn in my [the] flesh" in 2 Corinthians 12:7–10. He does not identify this "thorn" specifically, although his other letters hint that he may have been losing his eyesight. In Galatians 4:13–15, Paul remarks that the believers were so concerned about his condition that: "I can testify that, if you could have done so, you would have torn out your eyes and given them to me." He also often had others transcribe his words for him and, when he wrote himself, Paul sometimes made a special note suggesting that he had difficulty reading. "See what large letters I use as I write to you with my own hand!" (Gal. 6:11). Whatever the precise nature of this thorn in the flesh, Paul characterized it as "a messenger of Satan, to torment me" (2 Cor. 12:7) and explains that "three times I pleaded with the Lord to take it away from me" (2 Cor. 12:8).

Yet, despite his fervent prayers and faith, God did not take away his thorn in the flesh but instead declared: "My grace is sufficient for you, for my power is made perfect in weakness" (2 Cor. 12:9). Rather than becoming angry or resentful toward God for failing to relieve his suffering, Paul responded:

> Therefore I will boast all the more gladly about my weaknesses, so that Christ's power may rest on me. That is why, for Christ's sake, I delight in weaknesses, in insults, in hardships, in persecutions, in difficulties. For when I am weak, then I am strong. (2 Cor. 12:9–10)

To be clear, Paul was very familiar with God's healing power and, as recorded in the book of Acts, he healed others in Christ's name. As Paul and his companion Barnabas boldly proclaimed the gospel, the Lord "confirmed the message of his grace by enabling them to perform signs and wonders" (Acts 14:3), including healing a lame man (Acts 14:8–10), casting a demon out of a girl (Acts 16:16–18), raising a man from the dead (Acts 20:9–12), and curing the many sick brought to him (Acts 28:8–9). "God did extraordinary miracles through Paul, so that even handkerchiefs and aprons that had touched him were taken to the sick, and their illnesses cured and the evil spirits left them" (Acts 19:11–12). However, as apparent from Paul's own "thorn in the flesh," God sometimes calls us to grow through suffering.

Even if we never experience hardships like Paul, we need to be prepared to suffer for Christ's sake. And although God may answer our prayers to take away our thorns in the flesh, we also need to be prepared to praise God if we receive the same answer as Paul and discover the surpassing truth that "when I am weak, then I am strong" (2 Cor. 12:10). God can use a "thorn in the flesh"—whether a physical, emotional, psychological, family, relational or other challenge—to develop our character and drive us to ever-greater reliance on him.

CAN LIFE'S UP AND DOWNS SEPARATE US FROM GOD'S LOVE?

Absolutely not!

Paul is emphatic on this point when he asks: "Who shall separate us from the love of Christ? Shall trouble or hardship or persecution or famine or nakedness or danger or sword?" (Rom. 8:35). In response, he declares: "I am convinced that neither death nor life, neither angels nor demons, neither the present nor the future, nor any powers, neither height nor depth, nor anything else in all creation, will be able to separate us from the love of God that is in Christ Jesus our Lord" (Rom. 8:38–39).

We have the assurance of ultimate victory in Christ. "If God is for us, who can be against us? He who did not spare his own Son, but gave him up for us all—how will he not also, along with him, graciously give us all things?" (Rom. 8:31–32). God alone is in the position to decide our destiny. "Who will bring any charge against those whom God had chosen? It is God who justifies. Who then is the one who condemns? No one. Christ Jesus who died—more than that, who was raised to life— is at the right hand of God and is also interceding for us" (Rom. 8:33–34).

Can God be defeated? And if we are in him, can we be defeated? "No, in all these things we are more than conquerors through him who loved us" (Rom. 8:37). "And we know that in all things God works for the good of those who love him, who have been called according to his purpose. For those God foreknew he also predestined to be conformed to the image of his Son, that he might be the firstborn among many brothers and sisters. And those he predestined, he also called; those he called, he also justified; those he justified, he also glorified" (Rom. 8:28–30).

Even if we feel defeated at times, the spiritual reality is that we have the assurance of ultimate and eternal victory. "Though outwardly we are wasting away, yet inwardly we are being renewed day by day. For our light and momentary troubles are achieving for us an eternal glory that far outweighs them all. So we fix our eyes not on what is seen, but on what is unseen, since what is seen is temporary, but what is unseen is eternal" (2 Cor. 4:16–18).

Paul understood that life's circumstances—both ups and downs—can lead us astray. When things seem to be going badly, we can mistakenly assume that God is no longer taking care of us. And when things go well, we may imagine that we're doing a good job taking care of ourselves and that our possessions and worldly reputation will carry us to the end. Yet worldly success counts for nothing compared to the riches of knowing Christ, who alone can sustain us both now and through eternity. And it is precisely during the "downs" of life that God wants us to develop our characters and conform us to the image of Christ. Rather than being driven by circumstances, we can stand firm in Christ no matter what the circumstances.

WHAT DO PAUL'S INSTRUCTIONS MEAN FOR US TODAY?

Pause and reflect on how we deal with the ups and downs of life. Use the following questions to consider carefully Paul's instruction and example on this subject:

1. Do we feel tossed about by the ups and down of life? How does Christ empower us to stand firm under all circumstances?
2. Do we put our confidence primarily in our education, professional achievements, material possessions, social status, etc.? What will we do when they fail us?
3. Do we boast in the Lord or in ourselves? Why is pride so offensive to God?
4. What are our basic strategies for getting through difficult times? Are our strategies significantly different from the strategies used by unbelievers? Should they be different?
5. How does focusing on Christ help us get through difficult times? What does Paul mean when he declares that "I can do all this

[everything] through him [Christ] who gives me strength" (Phil. 4:13)?

6. What can we learn through difficulties? Is suffering always bad? What good can come from it?

7. What are some of the benefits of suffering? Have we experienced growth in Christ or other positive results from difficult times?

8. How does Paul's experience with suffering provide an example for us? What can we learn from his experience?

9. Do we fall into the extremes of either, on the one hand, trying desperately to avoid all suffering or, on the other, artificially creating difficulties for ourselves and others? What is the proper middle ground?

10. How do we need to change the ways we think and act to experience stability and victory during the ups and downs of life?

CHAPTER 10

Sexual Purity

Sex is viewed by many as a private issue not suitable for public discussion. Others treat it primarily as the subject of crude humor. For Paul, it is an important matter to be addressed in a straightforward and candid manner. Sex is a gift from God that, all too often, we misuse and pervert into something ungodly. Paul calls us to view and treat sex in the proper and balanced manner intended by God, and he won't let believers pretend to ignore it or make light of it.

WHAT IS GOD'S PLAN FOR SEX?

Sex is an important part of God's plan for marriage. As discussed further in chapter 11 of our study, the husband-wife union is intended to be the most intimate of all human relationships. "For this reason, a man will leave his father and mother and be united to his wife, and *the two will become one flesh*" (Eph. 5:31). With these words, Paul is quoting what God said when creating man and woman (Gen. 2:24) and what Jesus said when explaining the sanctity of marriage (Matt. 19:5). While becoming "one flesh" surely involves much more than sexual intercourse, its most obvious meaning involves sex. Paul makes this point when explaining why it is so absurd—so contrary to God's plan—to have sex with a prostitute. In 1 Corinthians 6:16, Paul states: "Do you not know that he who unites himself with a prostitute is one with her in body? For it is said, 'The two will become one flesh.'" This intimate union simply has no place outside of marriage.

Regarding sex within marriage, Paul speaks in surprisingly plain and direct terms. In 1 Corinthians 7:3–5, he explains:

The husband should fulfill his marital duty to his wife, and likewise the wife to her husband. The wife does not have authority over her own body but yields it to her husband. In the same way, the husband does not have authority over his own body but yields it to his wife. Do not deprive each other except perhaps by mutual consent and for a time, so that you may devote yourselves to prayer. Then come together again so that Satan will not tempt you because of your lack of self-control.

Paul is describing a relationship where the husband uses his body to please his wife, and the wife to please her husband. This is not the type of self-centered view of sex so prevalent in the world. A husband and wife are to have sex regularly except "by mutual consent and for a time" (1 Cor. 7:5). This is not the manipulative approach to sex also common in the world, where it is withheld in order to punish or coerce something from your spouse. Moreover, while sex for procreation is certainly part of God's plan (Gen. 1:28), Paul also makes clear that becoming "one flesh" is intended by God as a means by which the husband and wife satisfy each other's proper sexual needs.

WHY IS SEXUAL PURITY SO IMPORTANT?

Not only does sex outside of marriage violate God's plan for marriage, Paul also explains that, for a Christian, sexual immorality is different in kind from other types of sin. In 1 Corinthians 6:18–20, he instructs:

Flee from sexual immorality. All other sins a person commits are outside the body, but whoever sins sexually, sins against their own body. Do you not know that your bodies are temples of the Holy Spirit, who is in you, whom you have received from God? You are not your own; you were bought at a price. Therefore honor God with your bodies.

One of the greatest mysteries—and miracles—of our faith is that Christ dwells in each individual believer. In chapter 5 of our study, we discussed the mystery of "Christ in you, the hope of glory" (Col. 1:26–27), and that the body is a temple of the Holy Spirit (1 Cor. 3:16–17; 6:19). In the Old Testament, the temple in Jerusalem was the place where priests would come into God's presence to offer sacrifices and engage in other acts of worship. Because God is now present in all believers, Paul calls us to "offer your bodies as a living sacrifice, holy and pleasing to God—this is your true and proper worship" (Rom. 12:1). Paul seems to be saying that when we use our bodies for sexually immoral acts, we are defiling a place where God dwells. "The body, however, is not meant for sexual immorality but for the Lord, and the Lord for the body" (1 Cor. 6:13). "Do you not know that your bodies are members of Christ himself? Shall I then take the members of Christ and unite them with a prostitute? Never!" (1 Cor. 6:15).

WHAT IS GOD'S VIEW OF SEX OUTSIDE OF MARRIAGE?

Paul harshly condemns both sex between two people who are unmarried (which is called "fornication" in the King James Version translation of the Bible) and sex between a married person and someone to whom he or she is not married (called "adultery"). The NIV translation of the Bible commonly uses the term "sexual immorality" to cover both fornication and adultery. Paul also speaks directly about homosexuality (Rom. 1:26–27). In several passages, he lists sexually immoral people among those under God's judgment:

- "Do you not know that the wrongdoers will not inherit the kingdom of God? Do not be deceived: Neither the *sexually immoral* nor idolaters nor adulterers nor men who have sex with men nor thieves nor the greedy nor drunkards nor slanderers nor swindlers will inherit the kingdom of God" (1 Cor. 6:9–10).
- "The acts of the flesh are obvious: *sexual immorality*, impurity and debauchery; idolatry and witchcraft; hatred, discord,

jealousy, fits of rage, selfish ambition, dissensions, factions and envy; drunkenness, orgies, and the like. I warn you, as I did before, that those who live like this will not inherit the kingdom of God" (Gal. 5:19–21).

- "But among you there must not be even a hint of *sexual immorality*, or of any kind of impurity, or of greed, because these are improper for God's holy people. Nor should there be obscenity, foolish talk or coarse joking, which are out of place, but rather thanksgiving. For of this you can be sure: No immoral, impure or greedy person—such a man is an idolater—has any inheritance in the kingdom of Christ and of God" (Eph. 5:3–5).

- "Put to death, therefore, whatever belongs to your earthly nature: *sexual immorality*, impurity, lust, evil desires and greed, which is idolatry. Because of these, the wrath of God is coming" (Col. 3:5–6).

- "It is God's will that you should be sanctified: that you should avoid *sexual immorality*; that each of you should learn to control your own body in a way that is holy and honorable, not in passionate lust like the pagans, who do not know God; and that in this matter no one should wrong or take advantage of a brother or sister. The Lord will punish all those who commit such sins, as we told you and warned you before" (1 Thess. 4:3–6).

- Using a lesson from the Old Testament as an example of God's judgment, Paul states: "We should not commit *sexual immorality*, as some of them did—and in one day twenty-three thousand of them died" (1 Cor. 10:8).

In 1 Corinthians 5:1, Paul also confronts sexual immorality in the Corinthian church "of a kind that even pagans do not tolerate: A man is sleeping with his father's wife." He spends that entire chapter of 1 Corinthians condemning this conduct and calling on the church not to associate with a person who claims to be a Christian but engages in such sin. In 1 Corinthians 5:9–11, Paul provides clear instruction about dealing with sexual sin within the church:

I wrote to you in my letter not to associate with sexually immoral people—not at all meaning the people of this world who are immoral, or the greedy and swindlers, or idolaters. In that case you would have to leave this world. But now I am writing to you that you must not associate with anyone who claims to be a brother or sister but is sexually immoral or greedy, an idolater or slanderer, a drunkard or swindler. Do not even eat with such people.

Paul addresses sexual immorality in direct and harsh terms in the hope of bringing about repentance and restoration. Indeed, in 2 Corinthians 2:5–11, Paul talks about the restoration of an individual, quite possibly the same man condemned in 1 Corinthians 5:1 for sexual misconduct. In 2 Corinthians 7:10–11, he further explains:

Godly sorrow brings repentance that leads to salvation and leaves no regret, but worldly sorrow brings death. See what this godly sorrow has produced in you: what earnestness, what eagerness to clear yourselves, what indignation, what alarm, what longing, what concern, what readiness to see justice done.

Paul also makes clear that continued vigilance is needed in the area of sexual purity. Near the end of that same letter, Paul expresses concern that when he visits Corinth again "I will be grieved over many who have sinned earlier and have not repented of the impurity, sexual sin and debauchery in which they have indulged" (2 Cor. 12:21).

Paul never suggests that sex is shameful or sinful in and of itself. Indeed, the opposite is true. It is a God-given gift to be enjoyed. However, Paul knows that this gift *must* be enjoyed within the proper context of marriage. If we take sex out of its God-given place, it becomes a serious sin. In light of Paul's instructions and warnings, we need to appreciate the seriousness of sexual immorality and put an end to it in our lives. If we repent, we will be restored to the fellowship of believers and our right relationship with God, and sex will be returned to its proper place.

WHAT DO PAUL'S INSTRUCTIONS MEAN FOR US TODAY?

Pause and reflect on whether our lives and lifestyles conform to God's call to sexual purity. Use the following questions to consider carefully how to respond to God's call:

1. How do we view sex? Is it a gift from God to be enjoyed within the intimacy and commitment of marriage? Or is it something common and dirty? What is God's view of sex?

2. Within our marriages, do we use sex in a manipulative manner to get our way and to gratify our own desires? How does this approach to sex distort God's plan and undermine our marriages?

3. How is sexual immorality different from other types of sin? What does it mean that our bodies are a temple of the Holy Spirit? How does this fact affect how we view and treat our bodies?

4. Why is sex outside of marriage condemned by God? Why does the world often promote a different view of sex in opposition to God's plan? How have we bought into the world's plan rather than God's plan?

5. How can we limit exposure to the world's influences that promote the wrong view of sex? What do we watch on TV? What internet sites do we visit? Do we block inappropriate TV programs and internet sites?

6. Are you having sex with someone to whom you are not married? Are you prepared to repent and, with God's help, stop?

7. Are you using pornography? Are you prepared to repent and, with God's help, stop?

8. Do we tend to view members of the opposite gender as sex objects? How does this view undermine healthy relationships as intended by God? Are we prepared to repent and, with God's help, stop?

9. Do we have Christian friends of the same gender with whom we

can discuss these issues in a confidential and supportive manner? What are the benefits of these types of accountability relationships?

10. How do we need to change the ways we think and act in light of God's call to sexual purity?

PART III: RIGHT RELATIONSHIPS

We put the gospel into practice in the context of human relationships. And it is in that context that we encounter many of life's greatest challenges. Paul thus provides a wealth of guidance on how to build healthy relationships as intended by God. In chapter 11 of our study, we consider the foundational principles of love and service identified by Paul that should underlie all of our relationships. Rather than retreating from the difficulties of interpersonal relationships, Paul calls us to experience Christ—and growth in Christ—in the context of the family (chapter 12), the church (chapter 13), the world (chapter 14), caring for the needy (chapter 15), and personal friendships (chapter 16).

CHAPTER 11

The Foundational Principles of Love and Service

Love and service should define all of our relationships. As displayed by Christ himself, God's love goes hand in hand with service and sacrifice. Because Christ dwells in us (as discussed in Part II of our study), his character should be displayed in our lives. As we reflect Christ's character—most importantly, his heart of love and service—we discover the foundation on which to build healthy relationships.

WHAT IS THE ROLE OF LOVE IN A CHRISTIAN'S LIFE?

Love is the supreme virtue that brings together all other qualities of Christian character. Thus, after calling believers to "clothe yourselves with compassion, kindness, humility, gentleness and patience," Paul instructs: "And over all these virtues put on love, which binds them all together in perfect unity" (Col. 3:12–14). Love is listed first among the "fruit of the Spirit" (Gal. 5:22–23). In the concluding verse of 1 Corinthians 13 (often called the "love chapter"), Paul also highlights the supreme importance of love by explaining: "And now these three remain: faith, hope and love. But the greatest of these is love" (1 Cor. 13:13). "The only thing that counts is faith expressing itself through love" (Gal. 5:6).

Given the supreme importance of love, Paul instructs Christians to "follow the way of love" (1 Cor. 14:1). "Do everything in love" (1 Cor. 16:14). "Walk in the way of love" (Eph. 5:2. We should be "rooted and established in love" (Eph. 3:17). We should be "speaking the truth in love" (Eph. 4:15). "Be devoted to one another in love" (Rom. 12:10). "Be completely humble and gentle; be patient, bearing with one another in love" (Eph. 4:2). This call to love extends to every dimension of Christian life.

Our love for others should also be ever increasing. Paul prays: "May the Lord make your love increase and overflow for each other and for everyone else, just as ours does for you" (1 Thess. 3:12). He explains that "this is my prayer: that your love may abound more and more in knowledge and depth of insight" (Phil. 1:9). He thanks God for the church in Thessalonica because "the love all of you have for one another is increasing" (2 Thess. 1:3).

And after noting that they "do love all of God's family throughout Macedonia," Paul continues: "Yet we urge you, brothers and sisters, to do so more and more" (1 Thess. 4:10). This call to ever-increasing love, like our call to holy living, would be impossible apart from Christ. It is only in the context of a relationship with the God of love that we can experience godly and growing love for others.

Without this love, our lives count for nothing. Paul declares in 1 Corinthians 13:1–3 that:

> If I speak in the tongues of men or of angels, but do not have love, I am only a resounding gong or a clanging cymbal. If I have the gift of prophecy and can fathom all mysteries and all knowledge, and if I have a faith that can move mountains, but do not have love, I am nothing. If I give all I possess to the poor and give over my body to hardship that I may boast, but do not have love, I gain nothing.

If we don't see godly love growing in our lives, we have missed the mark. The Christian life is more than a belief in a few core truths. It is more than holy living. We now have a relationship with God who is love and, because the God of love is dwelling in us, we should be displaying his love to others. There is something wrong with our relationship with God if we lack godly and growing love.

WHY IS LOVE SO CENTRAL TO A CHRISTIAN'S LIFE AND RELATIONSHIPS?

Love is central because it is the fulfillment of God's law. In Galatians 5:14, Paul declares: "The entire law is fulfilled in keeping this one command: 'Love your neighbor as yourself.'" He elaborates on this point in Romans 13:8–10:

> Let no debt remain outstanding, except the continuing debt to love one another, for whoever loves others has fulfilled the law. The commandments, "You shall not commit adultery," "You shall not murder," "You shall not steal," "You shall not covet," and whatever other command there may be, are summed up in this one command: "Love your neighbor as yourself." Love does no harm to a neighbor. Therefore love is the fulfillment of the law.

In declaring this truth, Paul is echoing Christ's own words. When responding to an expert in the Jewish law who asked, "'Teacher, which is the greatest commandment in the Law?'" (Matt. 22:36)

> Jesus replied: "'Love the Lord your God with all your heart and with all your soul and with all your mind.' This is the first and greatest commandment. And the second is like it: 'Love your neighbor as yourself.' All the Law and the Prophets hang on these two commandments." (Matt. 22:37–40)

Jesus again spoke this truth in a similar exchange recorded in Mark 12:28–31. Both Paul and Jesus taught that love is the fulfillment of God's law.

Our love for others is also a testimony to the reality of our relationship with God through Jesus Christ. Paul calls us to: "Follow God's example, therefore, as dearly loved children and walk in the way of love, just as Christ loved us and gave himself up for us as a fragrant offering and sacrifice to God" (Eph. 5:1–2). "God's love has been poured out into our hearts through the Holy Spirit, who has been given us" (Rom. 5:5). Paul challenges us to "grasp how wide and long and high and deep is the love of Christ, and to know this love that surpasses knowledge" (Eph. 3:18–19).

Paul's letters are filled with reminders of God's love for us. For example: Romans 5:8 ("God demonstrates his own love for us"); Romans 15:30 ("the love of the Spirit"); 2 Corinthians 5:14 ("Christ's love compels us"); 2 Corinthians 13:11 ("the God of love and peace will be with you"); 2 Corinthians 13:14 ("the love of God…be with you"); Ephesians 2:4 ("his great love for us"); 1 Thessalonians 1:4 ("brothers and sisters loved by God"); 2 Thessalonians 2:13 ("brothers and sisters loved by the Lord"); 2 Thessalonians 2:16 ("God our Father, who loved us"); 2 Thessalonians 3:5 ("May the Lord direct your hearts into God's love"). We love because we have a relationship with a loving God.

The love of God for us, and thus our love for others, is not some fleeting experience or emotion. It is a constant reality from which no external force can separate us. In Romans 8:35, Paul asks: "Who shall separate us from the love of Christ?" After listing all sorts of troubles that you might imagine could separate us from God's love, Paul declares:

> For I am convinced that neither death nor life, neither angels nor demons, neither the present nor the future, nor any powers, neither height nor depth, nor anything else in all creation, will be able to separate us from the love of God that is in Christ Jesus our Lord. (Rom. 8:38–39)

Because love is at the heart of God's nature, our love for others is a natural expression of—indeed, an important part and proof of—the reality of our relationship with God. This truth is stated perhaps most clearly not in Paul's letters but in 1 John, which has been called the "epistle of love." "God is love. Whoever lives in love lives in God, and God in them" (1 John 4:16). "Whoever does not love does not know God, because God is love" (1 John 4:8). "We know that we have passed form death to life, because we love each other" (1 John 3:14). Because love is a defining characteristic of God, it should be no surprise that we believers are to constantly grow in love based on our relationship with the God of love.

WHAT DOES LOVE LOOK LIKE IN PRACTICE?

God's love is not the same as the world's often overly sentimental or sensual views of love. In 1 Corinthians 13:4–8, Paul provides perhaps the best known and most beautiful description of love on display in godly relationships:

> Love is patient, love is kind. It does not envy, it does not boast,
> it is not proud. It does not dishonor others, it is not self-seeking,
> it is not easily angered, it keeps no record of wrongs. Love does
> not delight in evil but rejoices with the truth. It always protects,
> always trusts, always hopes, always perseveres. Love never fails.

Consider how our relationships with family members, neighbors, coworkers, and friends—both believers and unbelievers—would be different if you demonstrated love as described in this passage. Consider also other passages in which Paul further describes the love God wants us to display. "Love must be sincere" (Rom. 12:9). "Love does no harm to a neighbor" (Rom. 13:10). "Knowledge puffs up while love builds up" (1 Cor. 8:1).

Love also expresses itself in forgiveness. Paul instructs: "Be kind and compassionate to one another, forgiving each other, just as in Christ God forgave you" (Eph. 4:32). "Bear with each other and forgive one another if any of you has a grievance against someone. Forgive as the Lord forgave you" (Col. 3:13). "Make sure that nobody pays back wrong for wrong, but always strive to do what is good for each other and for everyone else" (1 Thess. 5:15). Paul thus echoes Christ's own command that we forgive others as God has forgiven us (Matt. 6:12–15; 18:21–35; Mark 11:25; Luke 6:37; 11:4).

HOW DOES LOVE EXPRESS ITSELF IN SERVICE TO OTHERS?

Service and love go hand in hand. In Galatians 5:13, Paul instructs us to "serve one another humbly in love." In 1 Thessalonians 1:3, he thanks God for their "labor prompted by love." We will discuss later the call to diligent service in several specific contexts (the church in chapter 13, the workplace in chapter 14, and our care of the needy in chapter 15). But here, we will focus on the need for a servant's heart in general. Nowhere is this call to have a heart of service clearer than in Philippians 2:3–11 where Paul instructs:

> In humility value others above yourselves, not looking to your own interests but each of you to the interests of the others. In your relationships with one another, have the same mindset as Christ Jesus:

> Who, being in very nature God, did not consider equality with God something to be used to his own advantage; rather, he made himself nothing by taking the very nature of a servant, being made in human likeness. And being found in appearance as a man, he humbled himself by becoming obedient to death—even death on a cross!

> Therefore God exalted him to the highest place and gave him the name that is above every name, that at the name of Jesus every knee should bow, in heaven and on earth and under the earth, and every tongue acknowledge that Jesus Christ is Lord, to the glory of God the Father.

Following Christ's example, Paul repeatedly identifies himself as a "servant" (Rom. 1:1; 1 Cor. 4:1; 2 Cor. 6:4; Eph. 3:7; Phil. 1:1; Col. 1:23, 25). Since service and an attitude of submission should go hand in hand, Paul calls us to submit to governing authorities (Rom. 13:1, 5), to church leaders (1 Cor. 16:6), and wives to husbands (Eph. 5:22, 24; Col. 3:18). This call to submission is not limited, however, to a few specific relationships. In Ephesians 5:21, which is the verse immediately before his discussion of submission in marriage, Paul issues this general instruction to all believers: "Submit to one another out of reverence for Christ." We are *all* called to have an attitude of submission as Christians. Indeed, a rejection of submission is associated with a sinful mind. In Romans 8:7, Paul explains that "the mind governed by the flesh is hostile to God; it does not submit to God's law, nor can it do so."

Submission, which focuses on our heart's attitude, is not the same as simple obedience, which focuses on our actions. Thus, while Paul calls us to "submit" in the relationships noted above, he instructs children to "obey" their parents (Eph. 6:1; Col. 3:20) and slaves to "obey" their masters (Eph. 6:5, 6; Col. 3:22). To be clear, an attitude of submission clearly will affect our actions and, from the outside, it may look like simple obedience. However, submission is much deeper—and often more difficult—than obedience.

There also may be times when we can have a submissive attitude even while disobeying someone who is demanding that we do something wrong. When the apostles were commanded by governing authorities not to teach in Christ's name, their response recorded in Acts 5:29 was: "We must obey God rather than human beings!" A similar episode is recorded in Acts 4:18–20. Submission to human authorities is not the same as blind obedience. Throughout his writings, Paul makes clear that God alone is the final authority. Nowhere does Paul instruct us to obey human commands that conflict directly with God's commands. Yet even when standing firm in obeying God rather than man, we can display a respectful and submissive attitude to human authorities.

We should not imagine that a servant's heart is evidence of personal weakness. Jesus Christ, the most powerful person who ever walked the earth, provides the supreme model of a servant's heart. While words like "service," "servant," and "submission" may suggest a lowly status in this world, Christian service reflects a conscious decision to set aside our rights in order to give priority to the interests of others. A servant's heart reflects confidence in our standing before God as well as an understanding of things of eternal value, which puts in perspective the relative unimportance of what this world considers valuable.

Paul's own life also demonstrates that someone of great personal strength can have a servant's heart. From a human perspective, he had it all—well-educated, social credentials, and advancing far above his peers in his field. When he experienced the surpassing greatness and power of Christ in his life, he became a servant to all for the sake of Christ. However, he did not become a timid wallflower. He spoke powerfully and acted boldly as he served Christ by serving others. Like Paul, our lives can be marked by power and boldness as we serve and submit to others with Christ's heart of love.

WHAT DO PAUL'S INSTRUCTIONS MEAN FOR US TODAY?

Pause and reflect on whether love and service characterize our relationships. Use the following questions to consider carefully what it means to love and serve others:

1. Why is love the supreme Christian virtue? How does love fulfill all of God's commands?
2. How would our relationships be different if we displayed God's love toward others on a consistent basis?
3. How is our ability to love as intended by God affected by the truth that Christ and the Spirit dwell in us?
4. Does loving someone mean that we have to like the person or approve of the person's behavior? What is the difference between "love" and "like"?
5. What are the characteristics of love? In our relationships, are we patient? kind? protective of the other person's interest? trustworthy? hopeful? not envious? Or are we boastful and proud? rude, self-seeking and easily angered? a keeper of a list of wrongs?

6. How can we better display God's love to others? Is our love for others growing?

7. Are we committed to serving others? Why isn't service something to be avoided? Why does God call us to a life of service?

8. Do we put the interests of others ahead of our own interests? In practice, what does it mean to do so?

9. Does a servant's heart reflect personal strength or weakness? How do we view service? How does God view it?

10. How do we need to change the way we think and act if love and service are to be foundations on which our relationships are built?

CHAPTER 12

Family Relationships

Our faith is on display most clearly—and often tested most severely—within our families. In other contexts, we can hide many of our flaws and failures that are readily apparent to our spouses, children, or parents. Yet it is also within the family that we can experience God's love more intensely and intimately than in any other human relationships. While Paul does not suggest that family relationships will be easy, he does provide instructions and encouragement to experience the blessings and overcome the challenges of family relationships.

WHAT IS THE BASIC FRAMEWORK FOR A CHRISTIAN FAMILY?

In Colossians 3:18–21, Paul describes family relationships in pairs where each person has distinct responsibilities:

> Wives, submit yourselves to your husbands, as is fitting in the Lord. Husbands, love your wives and do not be harsh with them.

> Children, obey your parents in everything, for this pleases the Lord. Fathers, do not embitter your children, or they will become discouraged.

These distinct but complementary responsibilities are also found in Paul's discussion of family relationships in Ephesians 5:22 to 6:4. "Wives, submit yourselves to your own husbands as to the Lord" (Eph. 5:22). "Husbands, love your wives, just as Christ loved the church and gave himself up for her" (Eph. 5:25). "Each of you also must love his wife as he loves himself, and the wife must respect her husband" (Eph. 5:33). "Children, obey your parents in the Lord, for this is right" (Eph. 6:1). "Fathers, do not exasperate your children; instead, bring them up in the training and instruction of the Lord" (Eph. 6:4).

We might compare these family relationships to a dance. Dance partners move harmoniously together though each has different steps. Each person is responsible for his or her own steps, with the person in the lead providing direction with a gentle touch. Thus, rather than directing husbands to force their wives to submit, Paul calls them to love their wives and not be harsh. It is in this context where the wife can most easily perform her dance steps. To be clear, Paul does not relieve either party from his or her responsibilities despite missteps by the other party. The dance is best performed, however, when both move harmoniously with each focusing on his or her own steps.

The dance is also at its best when both are listening to the same music and performing the same dance. To continue this metaphor, God should be both the composer of the music and the choreographer of the dance. As Paul makes clear, God himself is to be a participant in each of these family relationships. Wives are to conduct themselves "as is fitting in the Lord" (Col. 3:18). Husbands are to love their wives "as Christ loved the church and gave himself up for her" (Eph. 5:25). Children are to obey their parents "for this pleases the Lord" (Col. 3:20). Fathers are to bring up their children "in the training and instruction of the Lord" (Eph. 6:4).

Paul describes healthy and balanced relationships within our families where we are all accountable for fulfilling our individual responsibilities, which will help other family members do the same. We thus can experience positive and productive family relationships as intended by God.

DOES GOD REALLY HAVE THE BEST PLAN FOR A FAMILY?

Some object that God's plan for the family is at odds with today's commonly held view that we should not differentiate between people based on gender and age. It is true that God does prescribe different roles and responsibilities within the family for husbands and wives, and for parents and children. In his omniscience, God understands that individual family members—as well as the family unit as a whole—thrive within the order that he has established.

Objections about the unfairness of roles based on gender and age also miss the bigger point that, as explained by Paul, God himself declares that differences based on gender, race and social status are irrelevant to a more important issue—our spiritual standing before God. For the purposes of the gospel, God does not view us based on the categories commonly used in our culture to divide people into different groups. In Galatians 3:26–28, Paul declares:

> You are all children of God through faith, for all of you who were baptized into Christ have clothed yourselves with Christ. There is neither Jew nor Gentile, neither slave nor free, nor is there male nor female, for you are all one in Christ Jesus.

Paul also speaks of the interdependence of men and women. "In the Lord woman is not independent of man, nor is man independent of woman. For as woman came from man, so also man is born of woman. But everything comes from God" (1 Cor. 11:11–12).

Paul never states that an individual's standing before God or responsibility for personal holiness depends on gender, age, or social status. The gospel can save and transform *everyone* regardless of the categories used by the world to separate us. Indeed, Paul declares the truth that "there is neither Jew nor Gentile, neither slave nor free, nor is there male nor female, for you are all one in Christ Jesus" (Gal. 3:28) at a time when society was much more segregated along those lines than today.

The unity amidst diversity in the early church (as discussed further in chapter 13 of our study) stood in contrast to divisions in the Roman world of Paul's day. Today, Christians, more than other people, should put aside our differences in light of the overriding unity that we have in Christ. In contrast to the false freedom of our culture, God offers true liberation in Christ!

WHAT IS GOD'S PLAN FOR MARRIAGE?

Paul affirms the plan for marriage declared by God at the time of creation (Gen. 2:24) and by Jesus when explaining the sanctity of marriage (Matt. 19:5) that: "'For this reason a man will leave his father and mother and be united to his wife, and the two will become one flesh" (Eph. 5:31). The unity and union intended by God for marriage goes beyond any other human relationship. Indeed, the marriage relationship is so special that, in it, Paul catches a glimpse of the mystery of the union between Christ and his church. He makes this connection in Ephesians 5:25–30:

> Husbands, love your wives, just as Christ loved the church and gave himself up for her to make her holy, cleansing her by the washing with water through the word, and to present her to himself as a radiant church, without stain or wrinkle or any other blemish, but holy and blameless. In this same way, husbands ought to love their wives as their own bodies. He who loves his wife loves himself. After all, no one ever hated their own body, but they feed and care for their body, just as Christ does the church—for we are members of his body.

Throughout this passage, Paul draws on the relationship between Christ and the church to explain how a husband should live sacrificially for his wife.

Similarly, when explaining why wives should submit to their husbands, Paul states in Ephesians 5:23–24:

> For the husband is the head of the wife as Christ is the head of the church, his body, of which he is the Savior. Now as the church submits to Christ, so also wives should submit to their husbands in everything.

Paul continues with this theme by stating: "This is a profound mystery—but I am talking about Christ and the church" (Eph. 5:32). He appears to address this mystery further in 1 Corinthians 6:16–17, where he compares the physical union between a man and a woman ("the two will become one flesh") with the spiritual union between Christ and the believer ("but whoever is united with the Lord is one with him in spirit").

Given the depth of the marriage union, as well as its similarities to the relationship between Christ and the church, it is not surprising that a Christian should be joined in marriage only to another believer. Paul's specific instructions about marriage in Ephesians 5:22–23, as discussed above, assume a commitment by both husband and wife to Christ and to live together in a manner that reflects Christ. A commonly quoted passage used to highlight the importance of marrying another believer is 2 Corinthians 6:14, where Paul states directly: "Do not be yoked together with unbelievers." Thus, when explaining that a widow "is free to marry anyone she wishes," Paul notes the important limitation that "he must belong to the Lord" (1 Cor. 7:39).

Later in this chapter, we will consider the potentially difficult issues of whether you should marry or remain single and what to do if you are already married to an unbeliever. However, the simple point here is that if you are single and decide to marry, God wants you to marry a person who is also a Christian.

God's plan for marriage contrasts with the commonly held view in our culture that tends to consider marriage as a convenience that, when it becomes inconvenient, can be abandoned. Marriage is not like a business relationship where each partner makes an investment and demands a good return. In God's plan for marriage, we are to become "one flesh" with our spouses, experience an intimacy and commitment found in no other human relationship, and display to others the mystery of Christ's profound love for his people.

SHOULD SINGLES REMAIN SINGLE?

Paul and possibly Barnabas were apparently the only apostles who were not married. When explaining the rights that he had forgone for the sake of his ministry, Paul notes: "Don't we have the right to take a believing wife along with us, as do the other apostles and the Lord's brothers and Cephas?" (1 Cor. 9:5). The "Lord's brothers" mentioned by Paul apparently included James and Jude who wrote the New Testament books bearing their names. And "Cephas" is another name for Peter (John 1:42) who, of course, wrote 1 and 2 Peter. Thus, as with the population generally, the common practice among the apostles and other church leaders was to marry.

Yet, while recognizing marriage as the norm, Paul says that it also can be "good" to be single. "Now to the unmarried and the widows I say: It is good for them to stay unmarried, as I do" (1 Cor. 7:8). Elaborating further on this issue, he explains in verses 26-27 of that chapter:

> Because of the present crisis, I think that it is good for a man to remain as he is. Are you pledged to a woman? Do not seek to be released. Are you free from such a commitment? Do not look for a wife.

To be clear, Paul is not *commanding* anyone not to marry. Indeed, when discussing his own unmarried status, he describes it as a gift that has not been given to everyone. "I wish that all of you were as I am. But each of you has your own gift from God; one has this gift, another has that" (1 Cor. 7:7). However, especially in light of the "present crisis" (verse 26), which is undefined in the text but apparently posed challenges for married people at that time, Paul saw clear benefits to remaining single. The benefits listed by Paul are worthy of careful consideration by those of us are not already married:

> An unmarried man is concerned about the Lord's affairs—how he can please the Lord. But a married man is concerned about the affairs of this world—how he can please his wife—and his interests are divided. An unmarried woman or virgin is concerned about the Lord's affairs: Her aim is to be devoted to the Lord in both body and spirit. But a married woman is concerned about the affairs of this world—how she can please her husband. (1 Cor. 7:32–34)

Once again, while noting the benefits of living "in undivided devotion to the Lord," Paul repeats that his encouragement to remain single is "not to restrict you" from getting married (1 Cor. 7:35).

Paul is also clear about circumstances when he counsels that we should marry. In blunt and direct terms, he instructs believers to get married if they otherwise would be burning with passion and drawn into the sexual immorality common in his time (and seemingly even more prevalent today). In his words, "it is better to marry than to burn with passion" (1 Cor. 7:9). Again, immediately after stating his general preference for remaining single, Paul states: "But since sexual immorality is occurring, each man should have sexual relations with his own wife, and each woman with her own husband" (1 Cor. 7:2).

While these particular statements about why to marry may seem rather negative, recall that Paul also discusses marriage in very positive terms—even revealing aspects of the nature of Christ's relationship with the church—as discussed earlier in this chapter.

Paul identifies great benefits both to getting married and remaining single. Having explained the benefits of both, Paul allows us to decide whether to marry in light of these biblical principles. If God is calling a believer to be single, this singleness should be for the Lord and not an opportunity to engage in a self-centered lifestyle. And if a single believer is falling into sexual immorality, that individual should consider again whether God is calling him or her into marriage.

WHAT ABOUT DIVORCE?

Paul also provides his typical blunt and direct instructions on the subject of divorce. In 1 Corinthians 7:10–11, he declares:

> To the married I give this command (not I, but the Lord): A wife must not separate from her husband. But if she does, she must remain unmarried or else be reconciled to her husband. And a husband must not divorce his wife.

This same instruction applies even if you are married to an unbeliever. In 1 Corinthians 7:12–13, Paul states:

> To the rest I say this (I, not the Lord): If any brother has a wife who is not a believer and she is willing to live with him, he must not divorce her. And if a woman has a husband who is not a believer and he is willing to live with her, she must not divorce him.

Paul does not suggest that marriage between a believer and unbeliever will be easy. Indeed, rather than identifying personal benefits to the believer by staying married to an unbeliever, he focuses on the benefits for the unbelieving spouse and the children of the marriage as key reasons to remain married:

> For the unbelieving husband has been sanctified through his wife, and the unbelieving wife has been sanctified through her believing husband. Otherwise your children would be unclean, but as it is, they are holy. (1 Cor. 7:14)

Further: "How do you know, wife, whether you will save your husband? Or, how do you know, husband, whether you will save your wife?" (1 Cor. 7:16). Peter makes a similar point when instructing wives to submit to their husbands "so that, if any of them do not believe the word, they may be won over without words by the behavior of their wives, when they see the purity and reverence of your lives" (1 Pet. 3:1–2).

Paul does not address under what circumstances divorce would be acceptable. However, without specifically mentioning divorce, he does make an allowance that: "But if the unbeliever leaves, let it be so. The brother or the sister is not bound in such circumstances; God has called us to live in peace" (1 Cor. 7:15).

Paul also does not address directly how these admonitions against divorce apply to a Christian who is already divorced. However, he seems to provide a clue to the answer in 1 Corinthians 7:17, where he instructs: "Nevertheless, each person should live as a believer in whatever situation the Lord has assigned to them, just as God has called them. This is the rule I lay down in all the churches." While this verse does not address specifically the issue of divorce, the underlying principle appears applicable to a Christian who is already divorced. We cannot live in continual regret over what already has happened and cannot be changed. While we can seek to correct past mistakes when possible, God meets us—and works with us—as we are today. For believers previously divorced, God deals with us as we are, as he does with every believer regardless of his or her baggage when coming to Christ. In Paul's words in another context: "Forgetting what is behind and straining toward what is ahead, I press on toward the goal to win the prize for which God has called me heavenward in Christ Jesus" (Phil. 3:13–14).

God's view of divorce is clear and stands in conflict to our culture's casual approach to divorce. Paul's instructions on divorce reflect this truth, yet he is also clear that God loves us where we stand today. And God stands ready to forgive and restore. These truths together provide the framework for our views and actions on the often sensitive subject of divorce.

WHAT INSTRUCTIONS DOES PAUL PROVIDE TO PARENTS AND CHILDREN?

Paul's instructions on the parent-child relationship are fairly brief and straightforward. Rather than attempting to address all of the different dimensions and dynamics of this relationship, he simply instructs children to obey their parents. "Children, obey your parents in everything, for this pleases the Lord" (Col. 3:20). "Children, obey your parents in the Lord, for this is right" (Eph. 6:1). He ties this instruction back to the Ten Commandments: "'Honor your father and mother'—which is the first commandment with a promise—'so that it may go well with you and that you may enjoy long life on the earth'" (Eph. 6:2–3).

Paul's instructions to fathers are only slightly more extensive, providing both positive direction and a negative admonition. On the positive side, fathers are called to bring up their children "in the training and instruction of the Lord" (Eph. 6:4). Paul is himself a role model for the training and instruction of "children" in the Lord. Paul often refers to those in the churches to whom he wrote as his children (1 Cor. 4:14; 2 Cor. 6:13; 12:14; Gal. 4:19; 1 Thess. 2:7, 11). Therefore, in a sense, Paul's instructions to the church in his letters provide a helpful model of how parents should train and instruct their children.

In addition to instructing fathers on what to do, Paul also admonishes them about what not to do. "Fathers, do not embitter your children, or they will become discouraged" (Col. 3:21). "Fathers, do not exasperate your children" (Eph. 6:4). To state the obvious: A discouraged or exasperated child is less likely to accept a father's training and instruction of the Lord or to obey his or her parents. Paul also apparently recognized a tendency with fathers—apparently more than with mothers—to embitter and exasperate their children. We fathers should take note.

These instructions on the parent-child relationship are far from a complete manual on how to raise children. As a practical matter, Paul leaves the parents themselves with the primary responsibility to decide how to raise their children. What works best in one culture may not be well suited for another. What works best in one family may not be best in another. Within the framework established by Scripture, Christian parents are left with broad responsibility to do what they believe best for their families after prayerful and thoughtful consideration.

We know firsthand that in our families, we can most fully experience the love of God on this side of heaven. Yet family can also be the source of the greatest testing and trial (and, by the way, of greatest growth). In our culture today, there is a wide range of conflicting models and views of family. However, as believers, we have a God-given model that does not change with the latest trends or theories. While we have considerable flexibility within the framework established by God, we risk losing many of the benefits and joys of family if we abandon God's plan for the latest fleeting—and failing—trends of today.

WHAT DO PAUL'S INSTRUCTIONS MEAN FOR US TODAY?

Pause and reflect on whether our relationships with our children, parents, and spouses are all that God intended. Use the following questions to consider carefully our family relationships:

1. Are our family relationships built on the principles of love and service that should be the foundation for all healthy relationships? How would our relationships with family members be different if we more fully displayed love and service?
2. Do we focus more on the other person's failures or missteps than on our responsibilities in the relationship? Is control more important to us than harmony? Is the image of a dance, as discussed earlier in this chapter, helpful to our consideration of healthy family relationships?
3. How does God's plan differ from the world's plan? Why is God's plan better?
4. Do the different roles prescribed by God within the family mean that some family members are more important than others? How

is the principle of equality consistent with differing roles within the family?

5. How do our different roles reflect the order that God wants for families? How would our families be different if they functioned as intended by God?

6. If you are single, should you get married? What are the benefits of remaining single? What are the benefits of marriage? If you are considering marriage, is your potential husband or wife a believer? Why is that important?

7. If you are a husband, do you love your wife and give yourself up for her? If you are a wife, do you have a submissive heart toward your husband? In practice, what do love and submission look like in a marriage?

8. If you are considering divorce, what does God want you to do? What is God's view of divorce? If you are already divorced, do you believe that God loves and receives you in your current situation?

9. If you are a child, how can you better honor and obey your parents? If you are a parent, how can you create an environment in which you are raising children to honor and obey you? Are you raising your children in the training and instruction of the Lord, or are you exasperating them with unreasonable and inconsistent instructions?

10. How do we need to change the way we think and act in light of God's plan for the family?

CHAPTER 13

Relationships in the Church

The church is the body of Christ. While we are saved as individuals and are individually responsible before God, we are also designed to live together in unity in local communities of believers. Together, we are more than our individual parts. Paul's letters are full of instructions on how, as a church, we can experience God's work in our lives and in the world in a way that surpasses our experiences as individual believers.

WHY DOES PAUL STRESS THE IMPORTANCE OF UNITY WITHIN THE CHURCH?

Christian unity is more than an abstract principle or feel-good emotion. In his letters to the churches, Paul identifies specific benefits to Christian unity in action. For example:

- "If you have any encouragement from being united with Christ, if any comfort from his love, if any common sharing in the Spirit, if any tenderness and compassion, then make my joy complete by being like-minded, having the same love, being one in the spirit and of one mind" (Phil. 2:1–2).
- "My goal is that they may be encouraged in heart and united in love, so that they may have the full riches of complete understanding, in order that they may know the mystery of God, namely, Christ, in whom are hidden all the treasures of wisdom and knowledge" (Col. 2:2–3).
- "May the God who gives endurance and encouragement give you the same attitude of mind toward each other that Christ Jesus had, so that with one mind and one voice you may glorify

the God and Father of our Lord Jesus Christ. Accept one another, then, just as Christ accepted you, in order to bring praise to God." (Rom. 15:5–7)

Thus, by living together in unity, we experience encouragement, comfort, tenderness, compassion, love, a better understanding of Christ, endurance, and acceptance—all to the praise of God.

Not surprisingly, in light of the many benefits, Paul repeatedly calls Christians to live together in unity. "I appeal to you, brothers and sisters, in the name of our Lord Jesus Christ, that all of you agree with one another in what you say and that there be no divisions among you, but that you be perfectly united in mind and thought" (1 Cor. 1:10). Again in Ephesians 4:3–6, he instructs:

Make every effort to keep the unity of the Spirit through the bond of peace. There is one body and Spirit, just as you were called to one hope when you were called; one Lord, one faith, one baptism; one God and Father of all, who is over all and through all and in all.

Not only is Christian unity beneficial to the life of both the individual believer and the church as a whole, it is also essential to the church's very identity as the body of Christ. In 1 Corinthians 12:27, Paul declares: "Now you are the body of Christ, and each of you is a part of it." He explains further in verses 12–13 of that same chapter:

Just as a body, though one, has many parts, but all its many parts form one body, so it is with Christ. For we were all baptized by one Spirit so as to form one body—whether Jews or Gentiles, slave or free—and we were all given the one Spirit to drink.

Similarly, in Romans 12:4–5, Paul explains: "For just as each of us has one body with many members, and these members do not all have the same function, so in Christ we, though many, form one body, and each member belongs to all the others."

Paul describes the church as a "body" more than thirty times in his letters to the churches. In 1 Corinthians 12 alone, he makes that comparison seventeen times. He also identifies the church as a "body" nine times in Ephesians (1:22–23; 3:6; 4:4, 12, 15-16, 25; 5:23, 29, 30), four times in Colossians (1:18, 24; 2:19; 3:15), and once in Romans (12:4-5). While the "body" is the most common image that Paul uses to describe the church, it is not the only one. "For we are co-workers in God's service; you are God's field, God's building" (1 Cor. 3:9). Paul also describes us as:

> fellow citizens with God's people and also members of his household, built on the foundation of the apostles and prophets, with Christ Jesus himself as the chief cornerstone. In him the whole building is joined together and rises to become a holy temple in the Lord. And in him you too are being built together to become a dwelling in which God lives by his Spirit. (Eph. 2:19–22)

There is a "mystery" in the relationship between Christ and the church. In part, this mystery concerns the unity of Christ and the church (Eph. 5:32). Further: "This mystery is that through the gospel the Gentiles are heirs together with Israel, members together of one body, and sharers together in the promise in Christ Jesus" (Eph. 3:6). Not only does this mystery concern our relationship with Christ and to each other within the church, part of this mystery is also that "through the church, the manifold wisdom of God should be made known to the rulers and authorities in the heavenly realms, according to his eternal purpose that he accomplished in Christ Jesus our Lord" (Eph. 3:10–11). In a way that we cannot understand, our unity as believers has a purpose and effect outside our present reality.

Our unity in Christ is tremendously important. Without it, we lose a key source of encouragement and many other benefits. We also cannot fulfill God's plan for the church as the body of Christ. We therefore need to give unity the same priority given to it by God.

HOW DO SPIRITUAL GIFTS PROMOTE UNITY WITHIN THE CHURCH?

Unity is not the same as uniformity. Indeed, we experience unity as Christians in large part because of our diversity. This truth is emphasized in Paul's discussion of spiritual gifts. "There are different kinds of gifts, but the same Spirit distributes them. There are different kinds of service, but the same Lord. There are different kinds of working, but in all of them and in everyone it is the same God at work" (1 Cor. 12:4–6). "Each of you has your own gift from God; one has this gift, another has that" (1 Cor. 7:7). Thus, as we begin our discussion of spiritual gifts, an important starting point is that God has given a diversity of gifts to believers so that, together, we can operate in unity as a church body. We need each other.

Our diversity and interdependence as Christians is highlighted in Paul's discussion of the church operating like a physical body. In 1 Corinthians 12:15–19, he explains:

> Now if the foot should say, "Because I am not a hand, I do not belong to the body," it would not for that reason stop being part of the body. And if the ear should say, "Because I am not an eye, I do not belong to the body," it would not for that reason stop being part of the body. If the whole body were an eye, where would the sense of hearing be? If the whole body were an ear, where would the sense of smell be? But in fact God has placed the parts in the body, every one of them, just as he wanted them to be. If they were all one part, where would the body be?

We are all important to the healthy functioning of a church body, and we all need each other. "The eye cannot say to the hand, 'I don't need you!' And the head cannot say to the feet, 'I don't need you!'" (1 Cor. 12:21). "If one part suffers, every part suffers with it; if one part is honored, every part rejoices with it" (1 Cor. 12:26). We should avoid trying to ascribe greater or lesser importance to particular members of the church body. As Paul explains in 1 Corinthians 12:22–25:

> Those parts of the body that seem to be weaker are indispensable, and the parts that we think are less honorable we treat with special honor. And the parts that are unpresentable are treated with special modesty, while our presentable parts need no special treatment. But God has put the body together, giving greater honor to the parts that lacked it, so that there should be no division in the body, but that its parts should have equal concern for each other.

When discussing spiritual gifts in Romans 12:3, Paul makes a similar point: "Do not think of yourself more highly than you ought, but rather think of yourself with sober judgment, in accordance with the faith God has distributed to each of you." Spiritual gifts are, by definition, something the Spirit has given us—not something that we have earned. Like the gift of salvation itself, we have no basis to boast (Eph. 2:8–9).

Perhaps most importantly, we should use the gifts God has given us to build up the church body as a whole. "Now to each one the manifestation of the Spirit is given for the common good" (1 Cor. 12:7). "Since you are eager for gifts of the Spirit, try to excel in those that build up the church" (1 Cor. 14:12). "When you come together, each of you has a hymn, or a word of instruction, a revelation, a tongue or an interpretation. Everything must be done so that the church may be built up" (1 Cor. 14:26).

"I long to see you so that I may impart to you some spiritual gift to make you strong—that is, that you and I may be mutually encouraged by each other's faith" (Rom. 1:11–12). After declaring that "Christ himself gave the apostles, the prophets, the evangelists, and the pastors and teachers," Paul explains that the role of these church leaders is "to equip his [God's] people for works of service, so that the body of Christ may be built up until we all reach unity in the faith and in the knowledge of the Son of God and become mature, attaining to the whole measure of the fullness of Christ" (Eph. 4:11–13).

Before we turn to Paul's discussion of particular gifts, it's important to remember the overall context of building up the body of Christ and promoting Christian unity. The primary purpose of spiritual gifts does not concern the individual believer. Spiritual gifts are vital to our life together in the church. We therefore need to exercise our gifts to build up the body so that we are a healthy and unified church.

WHAT ARE EXAMPLES OF SPECIFIC SPIRITUAL GIFTS?

Paul provides no single uniform list of all spiritual gifts. In Romans 12:6–8, he identifies several spiritual gifts:

> We have different gifts, according to the grace given to each of us. If your gift is *prophesying*, then prophesy in accordance with your faith; if it is *serving*, then serve; if it is *teaching*, then teach; if it is to *encourage*, then give encouragement; if it is *giving*, then give generously; if it is to *lead*, do it diligently; if it is to show *mercy*, do it cheerfully.

In another list of spiritual gifts emphasizing what some may consider to be "supernatural" (though, in reality, all God gives to his people is natural for him), Paul declares in 1 Corinthians 12:7–11 that:

> Now to each one the manifestation of the Spirit is given for the common good. To one there is given through the Spirit a *message of wisdom*, to another a *message of knowledge* by means of the same Spirit, to another *faith* by the same Spirit, to another gifts of *healing* by that one Spirit, to another *miraculous powers*, to another *prophecy*, to another *distinguishing between spirits*, to another *speaking in different kinds of tongues*, and to still another

the *interpretation of tongues*. All these are the work of one and the same Spirit, and he distributes them to each one, just as he determines.

A few verses later in 1 Corinthians 12:28–30, Paul provides yet another list that provides more of a description of the persons receiving the gifts rather than the gifts themselves:

And God has placed in the church first of all *apostles*, second *prophets*, third *teachers*, then *miracles*, then gifts of *healing*, of *helping*, of *guidance*, and of different kinds of *tongues*. Are all apostles? Are all prophets? Are all teachers? Do all work miracles? Do all have gifts of healing? Do all speak in tongues? Do all interpret?

This list has similarities to Ephesians 4:11: "Christ himself gave the *apostles*, the *prophets*, the *evangelists*, the *pastors* and *teachers*."

While Paul speaks much about spiritual gifts, he leaves many questions unanswered. He does not explain whether these lists are simply examples of some spiritual gifts or a comprehensive list of gifts when considered collectively. Nor does he address directly whether an individual Christian may have multiple gifts, or whether an individual's gifts may change over time or with need or context. Paul does not even provide detailed instructions on how you are to determine your spiritual gifts.

Paul is clear, however, that every believer has one or more gifts, that each of our gifts is important to the life of the church, and that we should use our gifts to build up other believers and the church as a whole. Rather than worrying excessively about spiritual gifts in the abstract, perhaps the most practical advice is that we ought to serve actively in the church and trust that God will equip us and use us for his service.

How can we overcome threats to Christian unity?

Christians confront many of the same divisive forces that plague all humans. Yet, as already discussed in Part I of our study, the believer is to deal with these divisions very differently from the unbeliever. In light of the surpassing importance of the gospel of Jesus Christ (chapter 1), we are to be united as one in Christ despite the differences into which the world categorizes people. "There is neither Jew nor Gentile, neither slave nor free, nor is there male and female, for you are all one in Christ Jesus" (Gal. 3:28). "For we were all baptized by one Spirit so as to form one body—whether Jews or Gentiles, slave or free—and we were all given the one Spirit to drink" (1 Cor. 12:13).

Moreover, as discussed in chapter 4, we are called to accept each other and respect the freedom that we all have in Christ. "Accept the one whose faith is weak, without quarreling over disputable matters" (Rom. 14:1). "Accept one another, then, just as Christ accepted you, in order to bring praise to God" (Rom. 15:7).

In Part II of our study, we considered the transforming work of Christ in our lives that gives us victory over our old sinful nature and empowers us to live holy lives—all of which promotes Christian unity. It is because of our new nature in Christ that we are able to forgive each other, serve each other, and be united to each other. In Colossians 3:12–14, Paul declares:

> Therefore, as God's chosen people, holy and dearly loved, clothe yourselves with compassion, kindness, humility, gentleness and patience. Bear with each other and forgive one another if any of you has a grievance against someone. Forgive as the Lord forgave you. And over all these virtues put on love, which binds them all together in perfect unity.

These virtues that promote unity remind us of the "fruit of the Spirit" in Galatians 5:22–23 discussed in chapter 5.

Further highlighting how these virtues promote Christian unity, Ephesians 4:32 instructs: "Be kind and compassionate to one another, forgiving each other, just as in Christ God forgave you." Again, in Philippians 2:3: "Do nothing out of selfish ambition or vain conceit. Rather, in humility value others above yourselves." We cannot simply manufacture Christian unity out of thin air. It flows from acceptance of the gospel, which provides the foundation for our unity, and from the transforming power of Christ in our lives, which draws us closer to our brothers and sisters as we all draw closer to Christ.

When potentially divisive disputes do arise within the church, we should be cautious about trying to resolve them through the world's processes. "If any of you has a dispute with another, do you dare to take it before the ungodly for judgment instead of before the Lord's people?" (1 Cor. 6:1). Paul expresses shock that "one brother takes another to court–and this is in front of unbelievers!" (1 Cor. 6:6).

In addition to reprimanding them for resorting to secular tribunals to resolve their disputes, he expresses grave disappointment both that a believer would engage in conduct that could give rise to such a dispute and that the wronged party would resort to legal recourse at all. "The very fact that you have lawsuits among you means you have been completely defeated already. Why not rather be wronged? Why not rather be cheated? Instead, you yourselves cheat and do wrong, and you do this to your brothers and sisters" (1 Cor. 6:7–8).

While we should pray that serious disputes do not arise between believers, if they do, they should be resolved within the church. Better to go to even a poor judge within the church than to a secular tribunal. "Therefore, if you have disputes about such matters, do you ask for a ruling from those whose way of life is scorned in the church? I say this to shame you. Is it possible that there is nobody among you wise enough to judge a dispute between believers?" (1 Cor. 6:4–5). Paul does not prescribe a specific process for resolving every type of dispute between believers. However, he is clear that we should not buy into the world's confrontational approach to dispute resolution. We are to be guided by principles of love, service and unity. While this does not mean that wrongs between believers should go uncorrected, it does mean that our approach and objectives will not be the same as what is used by the world's judicial systems.

WHAT ABOUT DENOMINATIONAL DIVISIONS WITHIN THE CHRISTIAN CHURCH TODAY?

Paul would likely be distressed by the divisions between Christian denominations that have developed through the centuries. Even in his day, Paul expressed concern about the tendency of some Christians to divide themselves based on allegiances to particular church leaders. In 1 Corinthians 1:11–13, Paul reports that "there are quarrels among you" and explains: "What I mean is this: One of you says, 'I follow Paul'; another, 'I follow Apollos'; another, 'I follow Cephas'; still another, 'I follow Christ.' Is Christ divided? Was Paul crucified for you? Were you baptized into the name of Paul?" Returning a couple chapters later to this issue of divisions among these believers, Paul reprimands them in 1 Corinthians 3:3–9 by declaring:

> You are still worldly. For since there is jealousy and quarreling among you, are you not worldly? Are you not acting like mere humans? For when one says, "I follow Paul," and another, "I follow Apollos," are you not mere human beings?

> What, after all, is Apollos? And what is Paul? Only servants, through whom you came to believe—as the Lord has assigned to each his task. I planted the seed, Apollos watered it, but God has been making it grow. So neither the one who plants nor the one who waters is anything, but only God, who makes things grow. The one who plants and the one who waters have one purpose, and they will be rewarded according to their own labor. For we are co-workers in God's service; you are God's field, God's building.

For "regular" Christians like you and me, there may not be much that we can do to change the current state of affairs at the denominational level. Moreover, many efforts at "unity" among denominations seem to have led to watering down the gospel itself in the name of tolerance. And churches that reject denominationalism altogether seem almost invariably to become their own denominations in practice.

However, we certainly can take steps as individuals and as local churches to put aside our differences on nonessential matters for the sake of Christian unity. We can build bridges to Christians of other denominations and when explaining our religious identity, focus on Christ and the foundation of the gospel on which all Christians must base their faith rather than on denominational differences. We thus can promote Christian unity that is so important to the growth of individual believers, to the health of the church, and to our witness in the world.

WHAT DO PAUL'S INSTRUCTIONS MEAN FOR US TODAY?

Pause and reflect on whether our relationships with other believers promote God's plan for the church. Use the following questions to consider carefully our relationships within the church:

1. Are our relationships with other believers in the church an important part of our lives? Are fellow believers among our best friends? What does it mean to be part of a church or community of believers?

2. What can we do to promote unity within our churches? What do we do to encourage, comfort, and build up other believers?

3. What is the difference between unity and uniformity within the church? How can believers be united in Christ despite our many differences (racial, educational, social, economic, etc.)?

4. What are your spiritual gifts? When you look at the lists of gifts in Paul's letters, can you identify one or more gifts that you seem to have?

5. Do we use our gifts for the common good and to build up the church? Are we more focused on ourselves or others when it comes to our roles and ministries in the church?

6. Are we open to the Spirit giving a gift to us that may be outside our comfort zone? What about gifts that seem "supernatural" rather than those that we might consider to reflect a natural talent?

7. Do we think of ourselves as more important, or less important, than others within the church? Do we believe that, as Paul teaches, everyone is important in the church much like each part of our physical bodies is important?

8. Do we provide positive reinforcement when we see others exercise their gifts? How can we better encourage others in connection with their gifts and ministries?

9. What do we see as threats to unity within our local churches and among Christians in general? How can we work for unity without compromising the essentials of the gospel?

10. How do we need to change the way we think and act in light of God's plan for the church?

Chapter 14

Relationships in the World

Paul's instructions on relationships in the world seem to flow from Christ's words that we are "not of the world" but sent "into the world" (John 17:16-18). In Part II of our study on holy living, we were challenged by what Paul said about not buying into the world's values. "Do not conform to the pattern of this world, but be transformed by the renewing of your mind" (Rom. 12:2).

In this chapter, we will consider Paul's instructions on what it means to be sent into the world. While some might want to disengage from the world or have a hostile attitude toward it, Paul will have none of that. He instead calls us to be model neighbors, coworkers and citizens. Unbelievers should look at us and be attracted by how we conduct ourselves. And when the opportunity arises, we should share the good news of Jesus Christ with them. We are to be Christ's ambassadors in both word and deed.

HOW SHOULD WE TREAT OUR NEIGHBORS?

We should do good to and, to the extent possible, live a peace with our neighbors. "Be careful to do what is right in the eyes of everyone. If it is possible, as far as it depends on you, live at peace with everyone" (Rom. 12:17–18). "Therefore, as we have opportunity, let us do good to all people, especially to those who belong to the family of believers" (Gal. 6:10). "Be wise in the way you act toward outsiders; make the most of every opportunity. Let your conversation be always full of grace, seasoned with salt, so that you may know how to answer everyone" (Col. 4:5–6).

Paul goes even further in describing how we should conduct our daily lives. "Make it your ambition to lead a quiet life: You should mind your own business and work with your hands, just as we told you, so that your daily life may win the respect of outsiders and so that you will not be dependent on anybody" (1 Thess. 4:11–12). In short, we should be model neighbors.

WHAT ABOUT THE WORKPLACE?

We also are to be exemplary employees who work diligently with a positive attitude. "Serve wholeheartedly, as if you were serving the Lord, not people, because you know that the Lord will reward each one for whatever good they do, whether they are slave or free" (Eph. 6:7–8). "Whatever you do, work at it with all your heart, as working for the Lord, not for human masters, since you know that you will receive an inheritance from the Lord as a reward. It is the Lord Christ you are serving" (Col. 3:23–24). We are to conduct ourselves in this manner "not only when their eye is on you and to curry their favor, but with sincerity of heart and reverence for the Lord" (Col. 3:22). "Obey them not only to win their favor when their eye is on you, but as slaves of Christ, doing the will of God from your heart" (Eph. 6:6).

If others work for us, we are to treat them in a fair and reasonable manner out of respect for God. "Do not threaten them, since you know that he who is both their Master and yours is in heaven, and there is no favoritism with him" (Eph. 6:9). You should provide for them "what is right and fair, because you know that you also have a Master in heaven" (Col. 4:1). As we've already seen, the gospel of Jesus Christ levels the playing field for all regardless of our social station. A higher position in the workplace certainly does not suggest a higher standing before God.

While our particular work settings may be markedly different from that addressed by Paul, he identifies enduring principles with practical application for us today. The "workplace" specifically addressed in Ephesians 6:5–9 and Colossians 3:22 to 4:1 concerned the commonplace practice in the Roman world of slavery. Many Christians were apparently household servants and, accordingly, Paul discusses the master-slave relationship along with the husband-wife and parent-child relationships in the household (Eph. 6:1–9; Col. 3:18 to 4:1). We may work in different types of workplaces, but Paul's instructions have practical application to where we are today.

Paul also provides blunt instructions about lazy workers. We all need to learn the value of hard work. In 2 Thessalonians 3:10–12, Paul also speaks harshly about laziness:

> For even when we were with you, we gave you this rule: "The one who is unwilling to work shall not eat." We hear that some among you are idle and disruptive. They are not busy; they are busybodies. Such people we command and urge in the Lord Jesus Christ to settle down and earn the food they eat.

Paul is equally blunt when confronting those who lived previously by dishonest means. "Anyone who has been stealing must steal no longer, but must work, doing something useful with their own hands, that they may have something to share with those in need" (Eph. 4:28).

Nowhere does Paul discuss strategies for advancement in the workplace or any "get-rich" schemes that allow us to lead lives of leisure. Instead, he emphasizes honest hard work that puts food on the table, allows us to share with the needy, and provides a model of diligence to all.

WHAT SHOULD OUR RELATIONSHIP BE WITH GOVERNING AUTHORITIES?

We might imagine that Paul would have a negative or even oppositional view of secular government. He had been arrested, beaten, put on trial, and imprisoned without proper cause (Acts 16:22–39; 21:33–36; 22:23–30; 24:1 to 26:32; 28:17–21). Yet, despite his firsthand experience with unjust governing authorities, Paul instructs: "Let everyone be subject to the governing authorities, for there is no authority except that which

God has established. The authorities that exist have been established by God" (Rom. 13:1).

Other Scripture repeats this same direction. "Remind the people to be subject to rulers and authorities" (Titus 3:1). "Submit yourselves for the Lord's sake to every human authority: whether to the emperor, as the supreme authority, or to governors, who are sent by him to punish those who do wrong and to commend those who do right" (1 Pet. 2:13–14). Not only are we to submit to governing authorities, we are also to pray for them. "I urge you, then, first of all, that petitions, prayers, intercession and thanksgiving be made for all people—for kings and all those in authority, that we may live peaceful and quiet lives in all godliness and holiness" (1 Tim. 2:1–2).

In Romans 13:2–7, Paul explains why we should submit to governing authorities. "Whoever rebels against the authority is rebelling against what God has instituted, and those who do so will bring judgment on themselves" (v. 2). Regarding the proper role of governing authorities as instituted by God, Paul continues in the next two verses:

> Rulers hold no terror for those who do right, but for those who do wrong. Do you want to be free from fear of the one in authority? Then do what is right and you will be commended. For the one in authority is God's servant for your good. But if you do wrong, be afraid, for rulers do not bear the sword for no reason. They are God's servants, agents of wrath to bring punishment on the wrongdoer.

In light of the role of government as intended by God, "it is necessary to submit to the authorities, not only because of possible punishment but also as a matter of conscience" (v. 5). Paul continues in the next two verses:

> This is also why you pay taxes, for the authorities are God's servants, who give their full time to governing. Give everyone what you owe him: If you owe taxes, pay taxes; if revenue, then revenue; if respect, then respect; if honor, then honor.

To be clear, Paul does not speak against seeking change when governing authorities perpetuate injustice. There also may be times when the dictates of a governing authority are in direct conflict with God's commands. The apostles responded in that type of situation by stating "We must obey God rather than human beings!" (Acts 5:29).

We also live today in a democracy where our system of government depends on the active involvement of the citizenry. Paul calls us to be good citizens, which, for us, allows for political activity and even proper forms of opposition to governing authorities. However, even within our political system, Paul's instructions ring true that we are to submit to the governing authorities (Rom. 13:1, 5), show proper respect and honor to them (Rom. 13:7), and fulfill our civic duties including paying taxes (Rom. 13:6).

WHAT IS OUR ROLE IN SHARING THE GOSPEL MESSAGE OF SALVATION WITH UNBELIEVERS?

In addition to displaying the gospel through our actions, we also need to share the gospel with our words. Unbelievers can be drawn to the faith by seeing Christians live as God intended, but they also need to hear the gospel message in order to make an informed decision about whether to accept it for their own lives. As Paul explains, "faith comes from hearing the message, and the message is heard through the word about Christ" (Rom. 10:17). Earlier in the same passage (Rom. 10:14–15), Paul asks:

How, then, can they call on the one they have not believed in? And how can they believe in the one of whom they have not heard? And how can they hear without someone preaching to them? And how can anyone preach unless they are sent? As it is written: "How beautiful are the feet of those who bring good news!"

In 2 Corinthians 5:18-20, Paul declares that we are Christ's ambassadors who have a ministry and message of reconciliation:

All this is from God, who reconciled us to himself through Christ and gave us the ministry of reconciliation: that God was reconciling the world to himself in Christ, not counting people's sins against them. And he has committed to us the message of reconciliation. We are therefore Christ's ambassadors, as though God were making his appeal through us. We implore you on Christ's behalf: Be reconciled to God.

The bottom line is that we must share the gospel in both word and deed. We are to be "blameless and pure, 'children of God without fault in a warped and crooked generation.' Then you will shine among them like stars in the sky as you hold firmly to the word of life" (Phil. 2:15–16).

WHAT IF SOME PEOPLE RESPOND NEGATIVELY TO THE GOSPEL MESSAGE?

While some will accept the gospel, and many will be positively influenced by our words and deeds, others will respond in a negative or even hostile manner. In that event, Paul calls us to: "Bless those who persecute you; bless and do not curse" (Rom. 12:14). "Do not repay anyone evil for evil" (Rom. 12:17). "Do not take revenge, my dear friends, but leave room for God's wrath" (Rom. 12:19). "Do not be overcome by evil, but overcome evil with good" (Rom. 12:21). Even when the gospel is being rejected, our godly reaction can continue to be a witness to the person who is rejecting the gospel at that time.

While we are responsible for our own conduct and attitude in dealing with others, we cannot dictate how others will respond. Chapter 9 of our study discussed that, as followers of Christ, we should recognize that suffering is a part of our Christian walk—and that we can experience comfort and growth from these challenges. "We share in his [Christ's] sufferings in order that we may also share in his glory" (Rom. 8:17). In Christ's own words:

If the world hates you, keep in mind that it hated me first. If you belonged to the world, it would love you as its own. As it is, you do not belong to the world, but I have chosen you out of the world. That is why the world hates you. Remember what I told you: "A servant is not greater than his master." If they persecuted me, they will persecute you also. (John 15:18–20)

WHAT DO PAUL'S INSTRUCTIONS MEAN FOR US TODAY?

Pause and reflect on our relationships with unbelievers. Use the following questions to consider carefully how God wants to work in these relationships:

1. What is our reputation among unbelievers? Could our unbelieving friends identify anything different about us based on our lives and lifestyles?

2. Do we display Christian virtues such as honesty, integrity, peace, kindness, and generosity? Do we also display other characteristics that are less admirable and attractive?

3. Does our speech reflect our faith in Christ? When we discuss what is happening in our lives, do we provide honest reports that include our spiritual lives? When the opportunity arises, are we prepared to share the gospel message?

4. Do we work hard and responsibly in our jobs? Can our coworkers and supervisors rely on us to do the right thing? When we supervise others, are we fair and reasonable?

5. Is climbing the business or social ladder important to us? Do we compromise our morals to get ahead in business?

6. How do we view our relationships with the world? Under what circumstances should we be separate from the world? When should we be actively involved in it? How do we strike the balance between being in the world but not of the world?

7. How do we respond when unbelievers are critical of our faith and our lifestyles? How should we respond?

8. What does it mean to be a good citizen of both God's kingdom and our country? What are our attitudes toward the government? What attitude should we have?

9. Do we show respect to governing authorities? Do we obey the laws? Under what exceptional circumstances should a Christian not obey a law?

10. How do we need to change the way we think and act in our relationships with unbelievers?

CHAPTER 15

Caring for People in Need

Paul is both a role model and a source of practical instruction on caring for the poor and needy. Paul explains that remembering the poor was "the very thing I had been eager to do" (Gal. 2:10). Thus, during his travels, he collected gifts to serve as "a contribution for the poor among the Lord's people in Jerusalem" (Rom. 15:26). Several churches joined in this effort (Acts 11:29–30; 1 Cor. 16:1–4). Paul was so determined to deliver their gifts to the poor in Jerusalem (Rom. 15:25–28) that he went there knowing that prison and hardship awaited him (Acts 20:22–23). When explaining his actions, Paul echoed Christ's words: "'It is more blessed to give than to receive'" (Acts 20:35). His instructions flow from his care for people in need.

> ## WHAT PRINCIPLES DOES PAUL IDENTIFY TO GUIDE OUR CHARITABLE GIVING?

We should give eagerly out of a generous heart. "Each of you should give what you have decided in your heart to give, not reluctantly or under compulsion, for God loves a cheerful giver" (2 Cor. 9:7). When speaking about the extraordinary generosity of the Macedonian churches, Paul observes:

> In the midst of a very severe trial, their overflowing joy and their extreme poverty welled up in rich generosity. For I testify that they gave as much as they were able, and even beyond their ability. Entirely on their own, they urgently pleaded with us for the privilege of sharing in this service to the Lord's people. And they

exceeded our expectations: They gave themselves first of all to the Lord, and then by the will of God also to us (2 Cor. 8:2–5).

Paul does not address directly the practice of tithing a tenth of our income. Nor does he prescribe any specific formula for the amount that we should give. Instead, as noted above in 2 Corinthians 9:7, he calls us to make that decision in our own hearts to give willingly and generously as a way to honor God. While Paul praises the Macedonian churches for giving beyond their ability, Paul makes clear that their gift was "entirely on their own" and beyond what he expected (2 Cor. 8:3, 5).

Elsewhere, Paul identifies principles of proportionality and equality in giving. In 1 Corinthians 16:2, he instructs that "each one of you should set aside a sum of money in keeping with your income." In 2 Corinthians 8:12–13, he further explains: "For if the willingness is there, the gift is acceptable according what one has, not according to what one does not have. Our desire is not that others might be relieved while you are hard pressed, but that there might be equality."

The principles identified by Paul for guiding our charitable giving thus include generosity, proportionality, and equality.

WHAT ARE THE BENEFITS OF GENEROUS CHARITABLE GIVING?

Giving benefits both the recipient and the giver. "Remember this: Whoever sows sparingly will also reap sparingly, and whoever sows generously will also reap generously" (2 Cor. 9:6). Paul continues in this same passage:

And God is able to bless you abundantly, so that in all things at all times, having all that you need, you will abound in every good work. As it is written: "They have freely scattered their gifts to the poor; their righteousness endures forever." Now he who supplies seed to the sower and bread for food will also supply and increase your store of seed and will enlarge the harvest of your righteousness. You will be enriched in every way so that you can be generous on every occasion, and through us your generosity will result in thanksgiving to God. (2 Cor. 9:8–11)

We also benefit when we give because when we find ourselves in a time of need, those whom we have helped may be in a position to help us. In Paul's words: "At the present time your plenty will supply what they need, so that in turn their plenty will supply what you need. The goal is equality, as it is written: 'The one who gathered much did not have too much, and the one who gathered little did not have too little'" (2 Cor. 8:14–15).

Yet another benefit of generosity is that it brings praise to God. When discussing the collection of charitable gifts in 2 Corinthians 9:12–15, Paul declares:

This service that you perform is not only supplying the needs of the Lord's people but is also overflowing in many expressions of thanks to God. Because of the service by which you have proved yourselves, others will praise God for the obedience that accompanies your confession of the gospel of Christ, and for your generosity in sharing with them and with everyone else. And in their prayers for you their hearts will go out to you, because of the surpassing grace God has given you. Thanks be to God for his indescribable gift!

If we give generously with a proper attitude, both the recipient and the giver will be blessed and God will be glorified.

> ## WHAT IS THE PROPER BALANCE BETWEEN INDIVIDUAL RESPONSIBILITY AND COMMUNITY SUPPORT FOR THE NEEDY?

While Paul strongly encourages compassionate and generous giving to those in need, he also emphasizes the importance of each person working hard to put food on the table (as discussed in chapter 14). He established the rule among the churches that "'the one who is unwilling to work shall not eat'" (2 Thess. 3:10). A balance therefore needs to be struck between individual accountability and community support. Perhaps the easiest case is when a believer is able but simply unwilling to work. Nowhere does Paul encourage support for the lazy. To the contrary, Paul indicates that we do a disservice by facilitating laziness. He instructs us not even to associate with someone who refuses to work in order to shame him into getting back to work. In 2 Thessalonians 3:14–15, Paul directs:

> Take special note of anyone who does not obey our instruction in this letter. Do not associate with them, in order that they may feel ashamed. Yet do not regard them as an enemy, but warn them as you would a fellow believer.

At the other end of the spectrum are people who are in dire need due to external circumstances beyond their control such as a natural disaster or human cruelty. When discussing giving to the needy in his letters to the churches, Paul appears to be focusing primarily on this type of situation. Not only had "a great persecution broke out against the church in Jerusalem" (Act 8:1), there was also a shortage of food due to famine (Acts 11:27–28).

As already discussed, Paul was actively involved in collecting contributions for the needy in Jerusalem, which is located in the region of Judea. Paul's instructions to the churches about charitable giving apparently relate in large part to this specific need of the Christians in Jerusalem.

Most needy people we encounter fall somewhere between the extremes of being just lazy and experiencing extreme hardship due to natural disaster or human cruelty. Paul does not provide specific instructions on precisely what to do in every situation where an individual is in need. However, in Galatians 6, he does identify guiding principles regarding the proper balance between individual accountability and community support. He issues two sets of instructions in this passage that initially may seem at odds, but, upon consideration, suggest this proper balance.

On the one hand, Paul directs: "Carry each other's burdens, and in this way you will fulfill the law of Christ" (Gal. 6:2). On the other hand: "Each one should test their own actions. Then they can take pride in themselves alone, without comparing themselves to someone else, for each one should carry their own load" (Gal. 6:4–5). The word for "burden" in the Greek language, in which most of the New Testament was originally written, suggests something large and potentially overwhelming. The word "load" suggests something smaller and more manageable. While we all have "loads" that we need to carry in our day-to-day lives such as work and family responsibilities, there are also times when there are "burdens" too large to handle without help from fellow believers.

This line is not always clear. Something can be a manageable load for one person but an overwhelming burden for another. Moreover, we may not have a complete or accurate understanding of someone else's situation. When uncertain about what to do, we should consider the fundamental principles of love and service as discussed in chapter 11 of our study. We also should remember that generosity is to be the norm. We are to be "generous on every occasion" (2 Cor. 9:11).

How did Paul encourage charitable giving?

It would be nice if fundraising could consist of a simple explanation of the principles of generosity discussed above and Paul's straightforward instruction to "share with the Lord's people who are in need" (Rom. 12:13). However, in practice, we often need to be encouraged or even pressed to share our material resources. In 1 Corinthians 16:1–2, Paul provides rather businesslike directions on collecting for the needy:

> Now about the collection for the Lord's people: Do what I told the Galatian churches to do. On the first day of every week, each one of you should set aside a sum of money in keeping with your income, saving it up, so that when I come no collections will have to be made.

This advice sounds like a financial planner's wise counsel to set aside regularly a portion of our income to achieve long-term financial objectives.

Elsewhere Paul resorts to a bit more pressure. At times, he suggests a moral obligation to give. When discussing in Romans 15:26–27 that the Christians in "Macedonia and Achaia were pleased to make a contribution for the poor among the Lord's people in Jerusalem," Paul explains:

> They were pleased to do it, and indeed they owe it to them. For if the Gentiles have shared in the Jews' spiritual blessings, they owe it to the Jews to share with them their material blessings.

In 2 Corinthians 8:7–11, Paul both sets high expectations and suggests the potential for embarrassment if our charitable giving falls short:

> But since you excel in everything—in faith, in speech, in knowledge, in complete earnestness and in the love we have kindled in you—see that you also excel in this grace of giving. I am not commanding you, but I want to test the sincerity of your love by comparing it with the earnestness of others. For you know the grace of our Lord Jesus Christ, that though he was rich, yet for your sake he became poor, so that you through his poverty might become rich. And here is my judgment about what is best for you in this matter. Last year you were the first not only to give but also to have the desire to do so. Now finish the work, so that your eager willingness to do it may be matched by your completion of it, according to your means.

He continues a few sentences later in 2 Corinthians 9:3–5:

> But I am sending the brothers in order that our boasting about you in this matter should not prove hollow, but that you may be ready, as I said you would be. For if any Macedonians come with me and find you unprepared, we—not to say anything about you—would be ashamed of having been so confident. So

I thought it necessary to urge the brothers to visit you in advance and finish the arrangements for the generous gift you had promised. Then it will be ready as a generous gift, not as one grudgingly given.

We may feel uncomfortable when we hear a fund-raising appeal even for a very good cause. It would be best, of course, if we gave generously when we became aware of a genuine and fitting need—even before being asked. However, if we do not act initially on your own, a little encouragement and even a bit of pressure might be in order. Without a reminder, we may forget about the benefits of generous giving and fall back into a self-centered rather than God-centered attitude toward our material resources.

WHAT IS OUR RESPONSIBILITY TO SUPPORT THE SPREAD OF THE GOSPEL?

When you support those in the ministry of the gospel, you fulfill God's command. "The Lord has commanded that those who preach the gospel should receive their living from the gospel" (1 Cor. 9:14). Your gifts also "are a fragrant offering, an acceptable sacrifice, pleasing to God" (Phil. 4:18). Paul explains in 1 Corinthians 9:7–14, and again in 1 Timothy 5:17–18, that ministers of the gospel have a right to financial support.

Paul singled out the Philippian believers for the gifts that they sent "more than once when I was in need" during his ministry in Thessalonica (Phil. 4:16). The financial gifts began "in the early days of your acquaintance with the gospel, when I set out from Macedonia" (Phil. 4:15). Paul rejoiced in their gifts (Phil. 4:10) not because he was looking for a gift, but because he desired that "more be credited to your account" (Phil. 4:17).

Paul's letters do not contain the types of financial appeals common today in many fund-raising letters from mission and other religious organizations. Although he had a right to financial support, Paul did not exercise that right (1 Cor. 9:12–15) because he did not want either to be a burden (2 Cor. 11:9, 1 Thess. 2:9, 2 Thess. 3:8) or for financial appeals to distract from the gospel (1 Cor. 9:12). He explained that "what I want is not your possessions but you" (2 Cor. 12:14).

We should not wait for a plea for help to support financially those who preach the gospel. They have a right to our support, and Christ commands that we provide it. While they may be willing to go without rather than impose on others, we should apply the principles discussed earlier of giving willingly and generously to support the spread of the gospel.

WHAT DO PAUL'S INSTRUCTIONS MEAN FOR US TODAY?

Pause and reflect on how we should provide care for those in need. Use the following questions to consider carefully how God wants us to respond to the needs of both believers and unbelievers around us:

1. Do we give generously to those in genuine need? What is our attitude when making a donation? Are we cheerful givers?

2. Are we also responsible givers? Do we consider the organization's or individual's situation and the credibility of their needs?

3. How do we decide to which organizations we should make charitable contributions? Should we focus our giving on Christian charities or on our churches? Given the limits of time and information, how do we make an informed decision?

4. What amount or percentage should we give on a regular and ongoing basis to charitable organizations? Given that Paul prescribes no mathematical formula, what principles should we use to decide an appropriate level of giving?

5. How should we respond to needy individuals whom we know? How about a person asking for money on the street? How about someone we know from our churches, neighborhoods, or workplaces?

6. In practice, how do we strike the balance between carrying each

other's burdens and each person carrying his or her own load (Gal. 6:2, 5)?

7. When is it appropriate to offer assistance other than money? When dealing with an individual, is it less awkward to offer a meal, a ride, friendship, or other non-monetary assistance?

8. What if we or our families are in need? Should we tell our pastors or other church leaders in a confidential manner? How can other believers help if they are unaware of the need?

9. How should we respond when we hear a charitable appeal? How do we respond to high-pressure tactics?

10. How do we need to change the way we think and act in connection with helping those in need?

CHAPTER 16

Personal Relationships

Paul's letters contain many personal greetings and stories. This "personal touch" reminds us that, in practice, we live out the gospel in the context of relationships. Just as God deals with us on a deeply personal level—knowing even the number of hairs on our heads (Matt. 10:30; Luke 12:7)—so we should cultivate deep personal relationships with other believers.

> ## WHAT DO PAUL'S PERSONAL GREETINGS IN HIS LETTERS REVEAL ABOUT THE IMPORTANCE OF INDIVIDUALS?

As we near the end of our study, we will consider the personal remarks found at the end of many of Paul's letters. He extends greetings and words of encouragement to dozens of brothers and sisters in Christ.

- In Romans 16:5–10, Paul greets twenty-six individuals by name. He begins with Priscilla and Aquila whom we know from other Scriptures (Acts 18:2, 18, 26; 1 Cor. 16:19; 2 Tim. 4:19) and whom Paul identifies as "my co-workers in Christ Jesus" (Rom. 16:3). Others we know only from this passage; and, in several instances, we know only their names.
- In Romans 16:21–24, Paul identifies eight additional individuals who were with him when he wrote this letter, who wanted to extend greetings to the believers in Rome. In Romans 16:1–2, Paul also commends a woman named Phoebe who apparently carried the letter to Rome on Paul's behalf.
- Paul not only extended greetings from Priscilla and Aquila in 1 Corinthians 16:19 (as well as from "the church that meets at their

house" and broadly from "the churches in the province of Asia"), but also in 1 Corinthians 16:10–12 he commends Timothy and Apollos who planned to visit the church in Corinth. He further singles out three workers in Corinth—Stephanas, Fortunatus and Achaicus—stating, "Such men deserve recognition" (1 Cor. 16:15–18).

- In Philippians 2:19–30, Paul provides personal details about both Timothy and Epaphroditus whom he planned to send to that church. Later in his letter, Paul makes a personal plea for resolution of a dispute between two individuals in the Philippian church: "I plead with Euodia and I plead with Syntyche to be of the same mind in the Lord. Yes, and I ask you, my true companion, help these women since they have contended at my side in the cause of the gospel, along with Clement and the rest of my co-workers, whose names are in the book of life" (Phil. 4:2–3).

- In Ephesians 4:21–22 and Colossians 4:7–8, Paul commends Tychicus who apparently carried Paul's letters to those churches. Tychicus was accompanied to Colossae by Onesimus (Col. 4:9), who was an escaped slave from that city and is the subject of Paul's letter to Philemon (the slave owner). Paul also extends personal greetings to "Nympha and the church in her house" (Col. 4:15) and instructs Archippus to "see to it that you complete the ministry you have received in the Lord" (Col. 4:17).

- In Colossians 4:10–14, Paul sends greetings from Mark and Luke—who wrote the gospels bearing their names—as well as from Justus, whom Paul identifies as one of "my co-workers" who "proved a comfort to me" (Col. 4:11); Epaphras, who apparently brought the gospel to Colosse (Col. 1:6–8); and Demas, who was a prisoner with Paul as recorded in Philemon 23 but who subsequently deserted him as reported in 2 Timothy 4:10.

We might wonder why these greetings, commendations and other personal comments are included in the Bible. After all, our study has focused on God's eternal truths that apply to all people at all times—not primarily on personal matters related to a few specific individuals. However, Paul's personal remarks highlight that these enduring truths have their application in the lives of specific individuals at specific points in time—including you and me, here and now.

We should follow Paul's example of valuing individuals by extending personal greetings and other personal touches that reflect how we value others as God values them. We also might consider whether our names would be worthy of mention as faithful workers for the gospel of Jesus Christ if an epistle were written to our church today.

WHAT DOES PAUL'S RELATIONSHIP WITH THE CHURCHES
REVEAL ABOUT THE NEED TO INVEST OURSELVES
IN THE LIVES OF OTHERS?

Paul's life provides a model of working diligently with people, often over long periods of time, for the sake of the gospel. Paul was personally involved in leading the people to Christ and in establishing most of the churches to which he wrote. In the case of the Ephesian church, after a short initial visit (Acts 18:19–21), Paul returned for a period of more than two years as recorded in Acts 19:8–10. He later met again with the elders of that church as recorded in Acts 20:17–38. In his instructions to these elders, Paul states in verses 27 and 28:

> For I have not hesitated to proclaim to you the whole will of God. Keep watch over yourselves and all the flock of which the Holy Spirit has made you overseers. Be shepherds of the church of God, which he bought with his own blood.

Further reflecting his personal and passionate concern for their continued growth in the faith, Paul's letter to the Ephesians includes a prayer that "you, being rooted and established in love, may have power, together with all the Lord's holy people, to grasp how wide and long and high and deep is the love of Christ, and to know this love that surpasses knowledge—that you may be filled to the measure of all the fullness of God" (Eph. 3:17–19).

This commitment and concern also can be seen in Paul's relationship with the other churches to which he wrote. In the case of the Galatians, the record in Acts suggests as many as four visits by Paul. In the case of the Corinthians, Paul's second epistle reports that he already had been with them twice and intended to return a third time (2 Cor. 12:14 and 13:1). During his first visit, "Paul stayed in Corinth for a year and a half, teaching them the word of God" (Acts 18:11). In the case of the Philippians, he visited at least twice (Acts 16:12–14 and 20:6), and he was imprisoned for preaching the gospel during his first visit (Acts 16:16–40).

In Thessalonica, "Paul went into the synagogue, and on three Sabbath days he reasoned with them from the Scriptures, explaining and proving that the Messiah had to suffer and rise from the dead" (Acts 17:2–3). While many believed, others opposed Paul and started a riot, which caused him to leave (Acts 17:5–10). Paul's commitment to these churches is all the more impressive because he made these trips, spanning many hundreds of miles, without the benefits of efficient modern modes of transportation.

Paul's personal care and concern are apparent even with the two churches that he had not visited prior to writing his letters to them (Romans and Colossians). He wrote to the Romans how "I long to see you so that I may impart to you some spiritual gift to make you strong—that is, that you and I may be mutually encouraged by each other's faith" (Rom. 1:11–12). "I have often been hindered from coming to you" (Rom. 15:22). While he did visit them, it was not as planned by Paul. He came as a prisoner under arrest for preaching the gospel, and he remained in Rome under house arrest for two years (Acts 28:16, 30–31).

It was during his time under house arrest in Rome that Paul apparently wrote his letters to the Colossians. Neither the book of Acts nor his letter to that church report that Paul ever visited Colosse. However, an individual named Epaphras—who was apparently instrumental in establishing the church in that city (Col. 1:6-8)—was a fellow prisoner with

Paul (Philem. 23) and they were together when Paul wrote his letter to the Colossians (Col. 4:12–13).

Paul's personal care for them is also apparent from his letter where he wrote: "We always thank God, the Father of our Lord Jesus Christ, when we pray for you, because we have heard of your faith in Christ Jesus and of the love you have for all God's people," and "since the day we heard about you, we have not stopped praying for you. We continually ask God to fill you with the knowledge of his will through all the wisdom and understanding that the Spirit gives" (Col. 1:3–4, 9).

In short, Paul's ministry provides a model of commitment and consistency in encouraging and supporting others to receive the gospel and grow in their faith. We should consider our own commitment to building relationships in light of Paul's example. Rather than friendships of convenience, we should work to build godly relationships that build up both others and Christ's kingdom.

WHAT CAN WE LEARN FROM PAUL'S DEEP AFFECTION FOR THE CHURCHES?

Repeatedly comparing himself to a parent in his love and care for the churches, Paul shares tenderly: "Just as a nursing mother cares for her children, so we cared for you. Because we loved you so much, we were delighted to share with you not only the gospel of God but our lives as well" (1 Thess. 2:7–8). He continues a couple verses later: "For you know that we dealt with each of you as a father deals with his own children, encouraging, comforting and urging you to live lives worthy of God, who calls you into his kingdom and glory" (1 Thess. 2:11–12). He displayed "the affection of Christ Jesus" (Phil. 1:8).

Paul's parental affection is also apparent in 2 Corinthians 6:11–13 where he writes: "We have spoken freely to you, Corinthians, and opened wide our hearts to you. We are not withholding our affection from you, but you are withholding yours from us. As a fair exchange—I speak as to my children—open wide your hearts also." Again in 2 Corinthians 12:14–15:

Now I am ready to visit you for the third time, and I will not be a burden to you, because what I want is not your possessions but you. After all, children should not have to save up for their parents, but parents for their children. So I will very gladly spend for you everything I have and expend myself as well. If I love you more, will you love me less?

Paul displays not only parental affection but also parental pride. "For what is our hope, our joy, or the crown in which we will glory in the presence of our Lord Jesus when he comes? Is it not you? Indeed, you are our glory and joy" (1 Thess. 2:19–20). "You yourselves are our letter, written on our hearts, known and read by everyone" (2 Cor. 3:2). "I do not say this to condemn you; I have said before that you have such a place in our hearts that we would live or die with you. I have spoken to you with great frankness; I take great pride in you. I am greatly encouraged; in all our troubles my joy knows no bounds" (2 Cor. 7:3–4).

We can hear the anguish of a parent in Paul's words of correction to the Christians in Corinth. After sharply rebuking them on several points in his first letter to that church, he explains in his second letter: "For I wrote you out of great distress and anguish of heart and with many tears, not to grieve you but to let you know the depth of my love for you" (2 Cor. 2:4). "Even if I caused you sorrow by my letter, I do not regret it. Though I did regret it—I see that my letter hurt you, but only for a little while—yet now I am happy, not because you were made sorry, but because your sorrow led you to repentance" (2 Cor. 7:8–9).

He also encourages us to show brotherly affection to each other. Paul exhorts believers to treat each other like family. When instructing his coworker Timothy, he states: "Treat younger men as brothers, older women as mothers, and younger women as sisters, with absolute purity" (1 Tim. 5:1–2). Paul himself refers to other believers as brothers and sisters nearly ninety times in his letters to the churches. Because we are part of God's family in Christ, we should treat each other as family.

Consistent with the close and personal bonds of family members, Paul encourages believers to: "Greet one another with a holy kiss" (1 Cor.

16:20). He uses these same words in 2 Corinthians 13:12 and very similar ones in 1 Thessalonians 5:26. While a "holy kiss" might not be within our comfort zones, it certainly highlights the type of personal affection that Christians should have for each other.

SHOULD CHRISTIANS HAVE ROLE MODELS?

While we are called to cultivate deep personal relationships with other believers, we also need to be aware of the risks. There are dangers, for example, in putting anyone other than Christ on a pedestal. Indeed, as discussed in chapter 13, Paul warns against excessive allegiance to particular church leaders (1 Cor. 3:5–9). At root, our unity is in Christ alone.

Yet Paul also recognizes the benefits of godly role models. As they follow Christ, we can pattern ourselves after them (and, in turn, become examples to others).

- "You know how we lived among you for your sake. You became imitators of us and of the Lord, for you welcomed the message in the midst of severe suffering with the joy given by the Holy Spirit. And so you became a model to all the believers in Macedonia and Achaia" (1 Thess. 1:5–7).
- "For you, brothers and sisters, became imitators of God's churches in Judea, which are in Christ Jesus: You suffered from your own people the same things those churches suffered from the Jews" (1 Thess. 2:14).
- "We did this, not because we do not have the right to such help, but in order to offer ourselves as a model for you to imitate" (2 Thess. 3:9).
- "Even if you have ten thousand guardians in Christ, you do not have many fathers, for in Christ Jesus I became your father through the gospel. Therefore I urge you to imitate me" (1 Cor. 4:15–16).
- "Join together in following my example, brothers and sisters, and

just as you have us as a model, keep your eyes on those who live as we do" (Phil. 3:17).

- "Whatever you have learned or received or heard from me, or seen in me—put it into practice. And the God of peace will be with you" (Phil. 4:9).
- "Follow my example, as I follow the example of Christ" (1 Cor. 11:1).

While Christ is our ultimate role model and the Scriptures are our standard for sound teaching, we also can look to mature believers to see how they put biblical truths into practice as they follow Christ. Paul points to the value of godly role models that help our spiritual walk so that, over time, we too become godly role models for others.

WHAT DO PAUL'S INSTRUCTIONS MEAN FOR US TODAY?

Pause and reflect on how we can build strong personal relationships. Use the following questions to consider carefully how we can be better friends:

1. Do we value our friends and our relationships with them? How do we communicate that fact to them?
2. Do we greet and thank others in a manner that affirms them and our friendships with them? Do we send personal letters or emails?
3. Are we developing friendships with believers that are advancing God's kingdom? Do we have a "team" view of Christian ministry?
4. Do we invest ourselves in the lives of others? Do we spend time with friends in a purposeful and constructive manner? Do we pray for them and with them?
5. Do we have mentors and friends with whom we can discuss challenges and opportunities that arise in our Christian walk?

Do we give thoughtful consideration to the suggestions and guidance that we receive?

6. Are we mentoring others who are younger in the faith and could use our guidance? What would it take to be a good mentor?

7. Are we part of a church or other community of believers with a mentoring program? If so, should we get involved in the program? If not, are there less formal ways for us to develop this type of relationship?

8. Can we have a role model without putting that person on a pedestal? How can we strike the right balance?

9. Do we view our churches as an extended family? Are we like fathers or mothers to younger believers? Do we treat older believers with respect and honor like our own parents?

10. How do we need to change the way we think and act in connection with personal relationships?

Your Own Study of Paul's Letters to the Churches

Now it's your turn. It is time for you to put Paul's instructions into practice. Paul's letters are not abstract works of theology. They provide instruction that we need to live gospel-centered lives. His letters should shape what you believe, how you behave, and how you build relationships.

It's also time to undertake your own study of Paul's letters to the churches with an eye toward practical application. This book has sought to present Paul's instructions faithfully and thematically for your consideration and application. However, I claim no special revelation beyond the words of the Bible itself. As you prayerfully read the Bible for yourself, God can open your eyes, mind, and heart to understand how these eternal truths apply to specific issues you are confronting today. Here are a few suggestions to consider as you continue to study Paul's letters to the churches.

PUT ASIDE YOUR FEARS THAT YOU ARE NOT UP TO THE TASK

Don't be intimidated by the prospect of studying Paul's letters to the churches. They were written to "regular" Christians during a time when the literacy rate and average educational level were considerably lower than today. In Paul's words: "We did not write you anything you cannot read or understand" (2 Cor. 1:13).

This is not to say that everything Paul says is easy to understand—or to apply. As Peter observed, Paul's letters contain "some things that are hard to understand, which ignorant and unstable people distort, as they do other Scriptures, to their own destruction" (2 Pet. 3:16). You should not expect to understand instantly and fully everything in Paul's letters. However, so long as you approach them honestly and prayerfully, they (like all Scripture) are "useful for teaching, rebuking, correcting and training in righteousness" and they will empower you to be "thoroughly equipped for every good work" (2 Tim. 3:16–17).

TAKE A FRESH LOOK AT PAUL'S LETTERS BY STUDYING THEM IN THE ORDER THEY WERE WRITTEN

Try reading them in the order in which they were written. While their precise dates cannot be determined definitively from the biblical text, they were likely written in the following order: Galatians (AD 48–49), 1 Thessalonians (AD 51), 2 Thessalonians (AD 51–52), 1 Corinthians (AD 55), 2 Corinthians (later in AD 55), Romans (AD 57), Ephesians (AD 60), Colossians (AD 60), and Philippians (AD 61).

Because we generally read Paul's letters in the order they appear in the New Testament's table of contents (which lists them from longest to shortest), the first book that you encounter is Romans, which is by far the most challenging of Paul's letters. The rewards of a thorough study of Romans are tremendous. However, even for biblical scholars, it can be a struggle to work through that letter.

An advantage of studying Paul's letters to the churches in chronological order is that you start with five other letters (Galatians, 1 Thessalonians, 2 Thessalonians, 1 Corinthians, and 2 Corinthians) before getting to Romans. Having worked your way through five other letters, you will have much-needed background with the substance and style of Paul's writings when you get to Romans.

LISTEN TO PAUL'S LETTERS READ ALOUD WITH A GROUP OF FELLOW BELIEVERS

During Paul's time and for many following centuries, most individual Christians did not have the privilege of reading Paul's letters for themselves. It was not until the invention of the printing press in the fifteenth century that "regular" Christians were in a position to read the Bible. The common and necessary practice for centuries was for the Scriptures to be read aloud in gatherings of believers. Thus, in 1 Timothy 4:13, Paul instructs Timothy to "devote yourself to the public reading of Scripture, to preaching and to teaching." This "public" dimension to the reading of Scripture is also apparent from Paul's instruction in Colossians 4:16 that "after this letter has been read to you, see that it is also read in the church of the Laodiceans and that you in turn read the letter from Laodicea." Again in 1 Thessalonians 5:27, Paul directs: "I charge you before the Lord to have this letter read to all the brothers and sisters."

We should thank God, of course, for the many benefits of the opportunity to read the Bible for ourselves. Yet, without diminishing the importance of personal Bible study, we also should recognize the benefits of gathering together to listen to the Bible being read aloud by others. There is a beauty to the spoken word, and, in many instances, themes and patterns are more easily discerned when we hear the Scriptures read aloud.

The public reading of Scripture is also an experience shared collectively with other believers. This shared experience of listening to Scripture together not only helps to provide a common point of reference for our life together in Christ, it also provides a foundation and framework for discussing together the meaning and application of Scripture to our lives.

In a small group of believers—perhaps in your home or church—you might take turns reading Paul's letters aloud. Perhaps each participant can read a chapter (or whatever amount he or she feels comfortable reading aloud) while others listen carefully. Your group's reading of Galatians should take about twenty-three minutes, 1 Thessalonians about twelve minutes, 2 Thessalonians about seven minutes, 1 Corinthians about an hour, 2 Corinthians about forty minutes, Romans about an hour and ten minutes, Ephesians about twenty minutes, Colossians about fifteen minutes, and Philippians also about fifteen minutes.

If you cover one letter in each sitting and split 1 Corinthians and Romans into three sessions and 2 Corinthians into two, you can listen to all of Paul's letters in fourteen sessions that average about twenty minutes. Even if you were to listen to Paul's letters straight through without taking a break (which is not recommended), the entire listening experience would take only about four and a half hours. Reading them aloud can easily become a part of a small group or Sunday school experience.

FOCUS ON PAUL'S MAJOR POINTS AND RECURRING THEMES

As you listen to the reading of Paul's letters to the churches, keep a pen and paper at hand. Listen for and write down major points and recurring themes. At least during your initial listening, do not try to write down every point made by Paul. Instead, try to focus on the overall flow of his letters. Imagine yourself as a member of the early church to which Paul wrote. Consider how you would have responded at an emotional level, a spiritual level, and a practical level.

When you come across a particularly meaningful or challenging passage, you might make a note to come back later to study that passage. However, you should resist the temptation to pause too often on specific passages. One of the major goals of this suggested approach is to listen for recurring themes and the overall flow of Paul's letters. If you pause too much, you may be less likely to pick up these themes and flow.

EXPECT INSIGHTS THAT HAVE PRACTICAL APPLICATION IN YOUR LIFE

You should anticipate that God will change your mind, heart and life through the reading and application of Paul's letters to the churches. "For the word of God is alive and active. Sharper than any double-edged sword, it penetrates even to dividing soul and spirit, joints and marrow; it judges the thoughts and attitudes of the heart" (Heb. 4:12). Your study of Paul's letters is different from an academic analysis of an ancient writing. Like all Scripture, Paul's letters are living words that can reach deeply into your thoughts and attitudes today.

Finally, let's end our time together in the manner of Paul. Now that we've studied his instructions on right beliefs, right conduct and right relationships, we close with Paul's words:

> So then, just as you received Christ Jesus as Lord, continue to live your lives in him, rooted and built up in him, strengthened in the faith as you were taught, and overflowing with thankfulness. (Col. 2:6–7)
>
> *Amen!*

For more information about *The Simplified Guide* and
how to order it for your Bible study group, please contact:
info@TheSimplifiedGuide.com

or

visit the website at www.TheSimplifiedGuide.com

To inquire about discounted pricing for bulk orders,
please contact Deep River Books at:
office@DeepRiverBooks.com